Ulcerative Colitis: Your Questions/Expert Answers

Andrew S. Warner, MD

*Chairman, Department of
Gastroenterology
Lahey Clinic
Burlington, MA*

Amy E. Barto, MD

*Director, Inflammatory Bowel Disease Center
Lahey Clinic
Burlington, MA*

JONES & BARTLETT
LEARNING

World Headquarters
Jones & Bartlett Learning
5 Wall Street
Burlington, MA 01803
978-443-5000
info@jblearning.com
www.jblearning.com

Jones & Bartlett Learning books and products are available through most bookstores and online book-sellers. To contact Jones & Bartlett Learning directly, call 800-832-0034, fax 978-443-8000, or visit our website, www.jblearning.com.

Substantial discounts on bulk quantities of Jones & Bartlett Learning publications are available to corporations, professional associations, and other qualified organizations. For details and specific discount information, contact the special sales department at Jones & Bartlett Learning via the above contact information or send an email to specialsales@jblearning.com.

The authors, editor, and publisher have made every effort to provide accurate information. However, they are not responsible for errors, omissions, or for any outcomes related to the use of the contents of this book and take no responsibility for the use of the products and procedures described. Treatments and side effects described in this book may not be applicable to all people; likewise, some people may require a dose or experience a side effect that is not described herein. Drugs and medical devices are discussed that may have limited availability controlled by the Food and Drug Administration (FDA) for use only in a research study or clinical trial. Research, clinical practice, and government regulations often change the accepted standard in this field. When consideration is being given to use of any drug in the clinical setting, the healthcare provider or reader is responsible for determining FDA status of the drug, reading the package insert, and reviewing prescribing information for the most up-to-date recommendations on dose, precautions, and contraindications, and determining the appropriate usage for the product. This is especially important in the case of drugs that are new or seldom used.

Production Credits
Executive Publisher: Christopher Davis
Special Projects Editor: Kathy Richardson
Production Editor: Daniel Stone
Manufacturing and Inventory Control Supervisor: Amy Bacus
Composition: Jason Miranda, Spoke & Wheel
Cover Image: Top Left: © Galina Barskaya/ShutterStock, Inc.; Top Right: © Jack Hollingsworth/Photodisc/Thinkstock; Bottom: © Feverpitched/Dreamstime.com
Printing and Binding: Edward Brothers Malloy
Cover Printing: Edward Brothers Malloy

ISBN: 978-1-4496-6565-4

6048

Printed in the United States of America
16 15 14 13   10 9 8 7 6 5 4 3 2 1

Ulcerative colitis is one of the most common forms of inflammatory bowel disease. Believed to be caused by an immune-mediated process, ulcerative colitis is characterized by inflammation of the colon, and potentially of many different organ systems throughout the body. Symptoms of inflammatory bowel disease range from mild to severe, and one-quarter to one-third of patients with ulcerative colitis eventually need surgery. Fortunately, many effective treatments are currently available, with new and potentially even more effective therapies on the horizon.

This book is intended to be a patient-oriented, practical guide about ulcerative colitis. The questions have been taken from questions we have been asked over the years by patients with inflammatory bowel disease. The answers are a compilation of the latest scientific information along with our own experience in treating inflammatory bowel disease. In essence, this book recreates a visit to the healthcare provider's office. It contains the questions you wished you had asked and many that you never thought to ask. We explore how inflammatory bowel disease is diagnosed and treated, complications, when to have surgery and the different types of operations performed, diet and nutrition, lifestyle, and reproductive issues and pregnancy. This book can provide you with important and useful information, as well as an in-depth understanding of the many facets and nuances of ulcerative colitis.

PART ONE

The Basics

What are ulcerative colitis and
inflammatory bowel disease?

How do you get ulcerative colitis?

Is ulcerative colitis contagious?

More . . .

1. What are ulcerative colitis and inflammatory bowel disease (IBD)?

Ulcerative colitis is one of the two most common forms of inflammatory bowel disease (IBD) (the other is **Crohn's disease**). Although the cause of IBD is unknown, it appears to be a result of disruption in the normal functioning of the **immune system**. The immune system is the body's natural defense system and works by protecting us against foreign substances that could potentially cause harm, such as viruses, bacteria, or even cancer. In ulcerative colitis, there is an abnormal response of the body's immune system, which affects the large intestine or colon (**Figure 1**). As a result, the intestines become inflamed—red, raw, and swollen. This **inflammation** can lead to a variety of symptoms, including abdominal discomfort, diarrhea, rectal bleeding, fever, and weight loss.

Ulcerative colitis covers a wide spectrum of severity. Some patients become very ill and debilitated, whereas others have symptoms that are mild and easier to control. Ulcerative colitis can also affect the joints, skin, and eyes and can lead to malabsorption and weight loss, kidney stones, gallstones, and many other ailments. The vast majority of individuals with ulcerative colitis need to take medication regularly, and one-quarter to one-third of patients with ulcerative colitis eventually undergo surgery.

2. How do you get ulcerative colitis?

Ulcerative colitis is considered to be an **immune-mediated inflammatory disease**. One theory proposes that ulcerative colitis is triggered by an infection, such as a bacteria or virus, with the inflammation continuing

Ulcerative colitis

A disease characterized by inflammation of the colon.

Crohn's disease

A disease characterized by inflammation of the gastrointestinal tract which can affect any area of the gastrointestinal tract.

Immune system

An internal network of organs, cells, and structures that work to guard your body against foreign substances, such as infections.

Inflammation

A process characterized by swelling, warmth, redness, and/or tenderness; can occur in any organ.

Immune-mediated inflammatory disease

A condition that results from abnormal activity of the body's immune system.

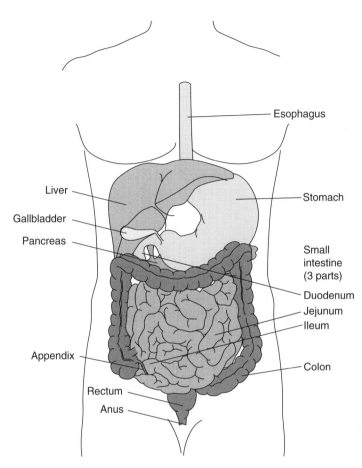

Figure 1 Normal gastrointestinal anatomy.

even though the infection has long since healed. This is known as **immune dysregulation**, or a failure of the body to regulate the immune system appropriately. Also, some people have a **genetic predisposition** to develop ulcerative colitis; research in this area is in its earliest stages.

If you have ulcerative colitis, it is important for you to realize that you did nothing to cause yourself to develop this disease, and you could have done nothing to prevent it. It's not from something you ate or didn't eat,

Immune dysregulation

Failure of the body to appropriately regulate the immune system; this lack of regulation is believed to be integral to the development of Crohn's disease and ulcerative colitis.

Genetic predisposition

An inherited trait that makes one more likely to develop a disease.

or from drinking too much alcohol or coffee, or from stress, working too hard, or lack of sleep. We simply do not know what causes ulcerative colitis. What we do know is how to diagnose and treat it.

3. Is ulcerative colitis contagious?

No. Ulcerative colitis is not contagious.

4. What is IBD and why is it called that?

Inflammatory bowel disease, or IBD, is a chronic disease of the gastrointestinal tract characterized by inflammation; Crohn's disease and ulcerative colitis are the two most common forms. Crohn's disease can affect any part of the gastrointestinal tract; ulcerative colitis affects only the large intestine or colon.

5. Is IBD the same thing as IBS?

No. Although there is only a one-letter difference in their names, IBD (inflammatory bowel disease) and IBS (irritable bowel syndrome) are two entirely distinct and different disorders. IBD is considered an intestinal disease; IBS, on the other hand, is what is known as a functional disorder (see **Table 1**). A functional disorder is not a true disease but rather a collection of subjective symptoms, such as diarrhea and abdominal pain, with no actual objective abnormalities found. So, while the subjective symptoms of IBD and IBS are similar, the distinction is that with IBD, objective abnormalities are found by laboratory, radiologic, or endoscopic testing, whereas with IBS all tests show normal results. This is not to say that IBS is not an actual disorder or that it's just in someone's head. IBS, much like a migraine headache, does have actual, physical symptoms, but without any objective findings, it cannot be classified as a disease. So, then, what is it?

IBS, as mentioned, is a functional disorder characterized by abdominal discomfort, diarrhea or constipation, sometimes diarrhea alternating with constipation, or a combination of these symptoms. Individuals with IBS are often classified as being pain-predominant, diarrhea-predominant, or constipation-predominant, depending upon the predominant symptom. The abdominal pain can be across the entire abdomen, or localized to one area of the abdomen (often the lower right or lower left side). However, some individuals with IBS may have just right upper side abdominal pain with no other symptoms. And although diarrhea is a common symptom, if one were to measure the total quantity of stool produced by someone with IBS over a 24-hour period, he or she would find that the actual stool volume was well

Table 1 Characteristics of IBS

Functional disorder
No objective abnormalities
Subjective symptoms
Atypical abdominal pain
Irregular bowel habits • Diarrhea • Constipation • Diarrhea alternating with constipation
Urgent bowel movements
Feeling of incomplete evacuation

within normal limits. So while subjectively a person with IBS may experience loose stool, the stool volume is actually normal. (Diarrhea is medically defined by stool volume and not stool consistency.) Along the same lines, individuals with constipation usually have normal **colonic transit time**, which is the amount of time it takes stool to travel from the beginning of the colon to the rectum. (Colonic transit time is determined by a test called a stool marker study. In this relatively easy-to-perform test, the patient ingests a capsule filled with approximately 20 radio-opaque markers that can be seen on a simple abdominal X-ray. If after 5 days, most of the markers are still in the colon, the patient has a delay in colonic transit. If no markers are present, the patient's colonic transit is normal. Colonic transit time is usually normal in people with IBS.)

Like IBD, IBS is a chronic disorder, and individuals with IBS learn to make appropriate lifestyle modifications. Because stress often exacerbates IBS, stress reduction is an integral part of therapy. Avoiding aggravating foods, such as fried and fatty foods and caffeinated beverages, is equally critical. If lifestyle modification alone does not control symptoms, individuals with IBS can take medications such as intestinal antispasmodics. However, unlike IBD, the mainstay of therapy for IBS should be lifestyle and dietary modification and not pharmacologic therapy. Patients with IBS don't usually develop IBD, but patients with IBD often experience IBS-type symptoms. Patients with IBD who suffer from IBS-type symptoms often experience relief with treatment aimed at the IBS symptoms.

Colonic transit time

The time it takes for stool to travel from the beginning of the colon (the cecum) to the rectum.

6. *How do you know if you have ulcerative colitis?*

Ulcerative colitis almost always presents with rectal bleeding or bloody diarrhea. When the inflammation is limited to the rectum, it is called **proctitis**. In patients with proctitis, bright red blood from the rectum or red blood coating a formed stool may be the only **sign** of rectal inflammation. **Proctosigmoiditis** is the inflammation of the sigmoid colon and rectum. When the inflammation extends up the left side of the colon, it is referred to as **left-sided colitis**. Inflammation that extends beyond the left side of the colon is called extensive colitis, or **pancolitis** (see **Figure 2**). In addition to rectal bleeding, individuals with left-sided or extensive colitis also have diarrhea and lower abdominal cramps, especially when they have to move their bowels. Patients with mild ulcerative colitis have less than 4 bowel movements per day, with or without blood. Patients with moderate ulcerative colitis will have 4 to 6 bowel movements per day. Patients with severe ulcerative colitis have more than 6 bloody bowel movements per day and show signs of fever and anemia (see **Table 2**). Some individuals also describe experiencing rectal spasm, which is called **tenesmus** and is caused by intense rectal inflammation.

Proctitis
Inflammation of the rectum.

Sign
Objective evidence of disease; a characteristic that can be identified on physical examination or by a test.

Left-sided colitis
Ulcerative colitis that involves the left side of the colon.

Proctosigmoiditis
Ulcerative colitis limited to the rectum and sigmoid colon, and not involving the descending colon.

Pancolitis
Extensive ulcerative colitis; ulcerative colitis that extends beyond the left colon.

Tenesmus
Intense rectal spasm, usually caused by inflammation.

THE BASICS

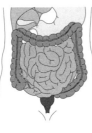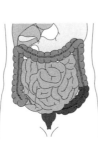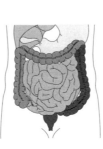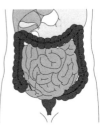

| Proctitis | Proctosigmoiditis | Left-Sided Colitis | Pancolitis |

Figure 2 Types of ulcerative colitis.

Colonoscopy

An endoscopic procedure in which a small, thin, flexible lighted tube with a camera on the end is passed through the rectum into the colon and, at times, into the ileum; an excellent test to detect inflammation and strictures in the rectum, colon, and ileum, and one that allows for a biopsy to be taken.

Biopsy

Usually performed during an endoscopy, a small piece of mucosa (inside lining of the intestine) is removed and examined under a microscope; an excellent test to characterize types of inflammation and detect dysplasia and cancer.

Sometimes it can be difficult to distinguish between ulcerative colitis and other diseases, such as Crohn's disease. This situation may occur when a patient has Crohn's disease involving the rectum and colon and presents with symptoms much like those of ulcerative colitis. In such a case, potential ways to distinguish between the two diseases include the following:

- Small bowel involvement—may be seen in Crohn's disease and is never seen in ulcerative colitis
- Appearance of ulcers on **colonoscopy**—Crohn's disease ulcers tend to be separate and are often very deep, whereas ulcerative colitis ulcers may flow together and are more superficial
- **Biopsy**—Crohn's disease has granulomas; ulcerative colitis does not.
- **Fistulas** and **perianal** abscesses—can be seen in Crohn's disease and are almost never found in ulcerative colitis.
- Blood testing—Crohn's disease is more likely to test positive for anti-Saccharomyces cerevisiae antibody (ASCA), whereas ulcerative colitis is more likely to test positive for antineutrophil cytoplasmic antibody (ANCA).

Table 2 Severity of Ulcerative Colitis

Signs and Symptoms	Mild	Moderate	Severe
Bowel movements	< 4/day	4–6/day	> 6/day
Blood in stool	Small	Moderate	Severe
Fever (°F)	None	< 99.5	> 99.5
Anemia	Mild	> 75%	≤ 75%
Rapid heart rate	No	< 90 mean pulse	> 90 mean pulse

7. Can someone have ulcerative colitis and not know it?

It is not at all uncommon for someone to have ulcerative colitis without knowing it. In fact, most patients with this disease have symptoms for months to years before they seek help. In these cases, the symptoms are usually mild enough so as not to interfere with the individual's ability to go about a daily routine.

It is common for individuals with proctitis to have rectal bleeding as their only symptom and mistakenly think that it is from **hemorrhoids**. Only by looking into the rectum would a physician be able to tell that the bleeding is actually from proctitis.

8. How common is ulcerative colitis?

Ulcerative colitis is not a common disease. Currently, it is estimated that approximately 1.4 million people in the United States have some form of IBD—either ulcerative colitis or Crohn's disease. Prior to 1960, ulcerative colitis was the more common of the two. Over time, however, the incidence of Crohn's disease has risen and now is nearly equal to that of ulcerative colitis. Currently, the **prevalence** (the number of people affected by a disease in a population at a specific time) of IBD is around 75 to 150 cases per 100,000 people. Ulcerative colitis is more commonly found in developed countries and in northern latitudes, and less commonly found in less industrialized countries and in more temperate climates. Also, more often ulcerative colitis is seen in urban settings and less frequently found in more rural environments.

Perianal

The area adjacent to the outside of the anus; common site for abscess and fistula formation.

Fistula

A tunnel connecting two structures that are not normally connected; examples include a fistula between the rectum and vagina (rectovaginal fistula) or the colon and bladder (colovesicular fistula).

Hemorrhoids

Engorged veins found in and around the rectum and anus. Often they bleed and can cause rectal pain if blood becomes clotted within the hemorrhoids, which is a condition called thrombosed hemorrhoids.

Prevalence

The number of people affected by a disease in a population at a specific time.

THE BASICS

9

The peak onset of ulcerative colitis usually occurs in late adolescence and extends to early adulthood (ages 15 to 30 years), but a person can be diagnosed with the disease at any age—and it seems to occur equally in males and females. Ulcerative colitis occurs more often in those of Jewish decent, with Ashkenazi Jews having the highest prevalence.

9. What role does inflammation play in ulcerative colitis?

Inflammation—meaning soreness, irritation, and swelling—of the colon is the main characteristic of ulcerative colitis. Without the presence of this intestinal inflammation, your gastroenterologist may suspect you have a condition other than ulcerative colitis, such as IBS.

When your body has ulcerative colitis, molecules released by the immune cells in response to a perceived threat to the immune system cause inflammation in the lining of the colon, which can lead to ulceration, and ultimately scarring (also called fibrosis). The inflammation can be felt as abdominal discomfort or diarrhea, which can range from mild in some individuals to severe in others.

10. Is inflammation responsible for my symptoms?

The inflammation of ulcerative colitis is responsible for the abdominal discomfort you feel and can also cause other symptoms. Inflammation can cause scar tissue to build up in the colon over time and may cause a stricture to develop.

It is important, however, to note that inflammation does not affect just the lining of the colon. The inflammatory cells circulating in the body can cause many other symptoms that may seem unrelated to the intestinal inflammation. Question 35 addresses these other symptoms.

11. If I can reduce the inflammation, will I get better?

While ulcerative colitis is a lifelong disorder, the good news is that there are medications available to help treat the inflammation of ulcerative colitis. Treating the inflammation along with learning how to modify your diet and lifestyle has allowed many individuals with ulcerative colitis to get their disease under control. This may mean monitoring your symptoms, changing your diet, reducing stress in your life, or talking to your gastroenterologist about maximizing treatment to reduce inflammation.

12. Am I more likely to get colon cancer if I have ulcerative colitis?

If you have ulcerative colitis, you may be at an increased risk for developing colon cancer as compared to the general population. The two principal factors that determine your degree of risk are how long you have had ulcerative colitis and how much of your colon is involved (see **Table 3**). The greater amount of time you have had ulcerative colitis and the greater the extent of colonic involvement, the greater the likelihood that colon cancer will develop. Additional risk factors are **primary sclerosing cholangitis (PCS)**, which is a liver disorder that is associated with ulcerative colitis, family

Primary sclerosing cholangitis (PCS)
Inflammation and scarring of the bile ducts within the liver; can occur in ulcerative colitis and Crohn's disease.

Table 3 Risk Factors for Cancer in Ulcerative Colitis

Duration of disease
Extent of disease
Primary sclerosing cholangitis
Family history of colon cancer (immediate relative)
Activity of disease (possible risk factor)

history of colon cancer (immediate relation), and, possibly, activity of disease. It should also be clearly stated that although individuals with ulcerative colitis are considered to be at increased risk, this is as compared to the general population in which the chance of getting colon cancer in a person's lifetime is approximately 1 in 20. Although having ulcerative colitis does place you at increased risk as compared to someone who does not have ulcerative colitis, the majority of patients with ulcerative colitis still will not develop colon cancer.

A direct relationship exists between the amount of time you have had ulcerative colitis and the likelihood that cancer will develop. Studies show that the risk of colon cancer in ulcerative colitis is likely to be approximately 8% at 20 years and 18% at 30 years. It is recommended that people with ulcerative colitis have more frequent colonoscopies than the average population because of this increased cancer risk. The recommendation is to start these colonoscopies 8-10 years after the diagnosis of ulcerative colitis. They should happen initially every several years, more frequently as time goes on.

Another risk factor is the extent of colonic involvement. When ulcerative colitis is limited to the rectum, there does not seem to be an increased risk of cancer. The risk increases the farther up the inflammation extends into the colon and is highest when the entire colon is involved.

13. Can I do anything to prevent getting colon cancer?

Some scientific evidence indicates that long-term medical therapy with aminosalicylates may reduce the likelihood of developing colon cancer in ulcerative colitis. It is thought that chronic suppression of inflammation may inhibit the transformation of normal cells into **dysplastic cells**. Although the available data regard only aminosalicylates and no other drugs used to treat ulcerative colitis, many healthcare providers extend these findings to immune-modulating therapy as well. Also, there are some suggestions in the medical literature that nutritional therapy with folic acid and calcium may be protective, but this is "softer" data and the results may simply be based on chance occurrence.

Dysplastic cells
Cells that are in a state of abnormal growth or development.

PART TWO

Diagnosis

How is ulcerative colitis diagnosed?

Is ulcerative colitis ever confused
with other disorders?

Can I ever be cured of ulcerative colitis,
or will I have it for my entire life?

More . . .

14. How is ulcerative colitis diagnosed?

No one test can definitively diagnose someone as having ulcerative colitis with 100% certainty. Ulcerative colitis is diagnosed based upon a patient's clinical history and physical examination in combination with radiologic, endoscopic, and laboratory testing. And because each patient is an individual, not all patients undergo an identical evaluation; testing is tailored to each patient. Following are descriptions of some of the various tests that are used in the evaluation of IBD.

Radiology

- **Abdominal X-ray**

  Provides a picture of structures and organs in the abdomen and is helpful in detecting a bowel obstruction or **perforation**.

- **CT scan**

  Uses X-rays to create a more detailed look inside the body. A computed tomography (CT) scan is especially helpful in detecting an **abscess** and also is useful in evaluating for inflammation, bowel obstruction, or perforation. CT enterography is a type of CT scan that focuses on the gastrointestinal tract.

- **Upper GI series/upper GI series with small bowel follow-through**

  Allows a close examination of the esophagus, stomach, duodenum, and small bowel. The patient must drink a thick, white liquid barium shake, and then is X-rayed as the material travels through the gastrointestinal tract. This is an excellent test to help detect strictures, fistulas, and inflammation in the stomach and small bowel.

Perforation

A rupture or abnormal opening of the intestine that allows intestinal contents to escape into the abdominal cavity.

Abscess

A walled-off collection of pus; in Crohn's disease, an abscess is most commonly found around the anus or rectum, but can occur anywhere in the body.

- **Enteroclysis**

  Provides a detailed examination of the small bowel by passing a small tube through the nose, into the stomach, and into the **duodenum**; barium is then introduced through the tube directly into the small bowel. This is an excellent test to help detect minor abnormalities in the small intestine that might not be seen on an upper GI series with small bowel follow-through.

- **Barium enema**

  Allows a close examination of the rectum and colon by introducing barium through the rectum and taking X-rays as it travels through the colon. This is an excellent test to help detect strictures, inflammation, and fistulas in the colon.

- **Ultrasound**

  Uses sound waves to examine abdominal and pelvic organs; commonly used to look for gallstones and obstruction of the **bile duct**.

- **MRI**

  Uses a magnetic field to create a detailed picture of the structures and organs in the abdomen and pelvis. Magnetic resonance imaging (MRI) is especially helpful in detecting abdominal and pelvic abscesses; it can also be used to evaluate the bile duct and pancreatic duct.

- **Virtual colonoscopy**

  A CT scan of the colon used as a screening test for colon cancer as an alternative to endoscopy. This is increasingly being used, although it is unclear at present whether this is a better test than colonoscopy.

Duodenum

The first part of the small intestine just beyond the stomach.

Bile duct

A channel through which bile flows from the liver to the intestines.

Endoscopy

Endoscopy is a broad term that includes a variety of endoscopic tests, including **upper endoscopy** and colonoscopy. Prior to an endoscopic procedure, the patient receives a set of instructions describing the procedure in detail, including any preparations that may need to be made. All endoscopic procedures require a period of fasting beforehand. Some procedures require a colon prep, which involves flushing out the colon by way of liquid laxatives and ingestion of lots of fluids. Most but not all of these procedures are performed under **sedation**, which is administered intravenously. The sedatives do not make a patient completely unconscious, but rather induce a twilight state in which the patient is comfortable and sleepy. A patient will often entirely forget that the procedure has taken place and wake up at the end of the procedure asking, "When are you going to get started?"

Each of the following procedures (except capsule endoscopy) is performed using an endoscope (in the case of colonoscopy, the tool is called a colonoscope; see **Figure 3**). An endoscope is a small, thin, flexible tube (about the

Upper endoscopy

A procedure in which a small, thin, flexible, lighted tube with a camera on the end is passed through the mouth into the esophagus, stomach, and duodenum; an excellent test to detect inflammation and strictures in the upper gastrointestinal tract that allows a biopsy to be taken.

Sedation

Also called conscious sedation, or moderate sedation; sedation is a form of moderate anesthesia in which the patient is given medication to induce a state of relaxation. Patients under sedation are sleepy and are less likely to feel discomfort.

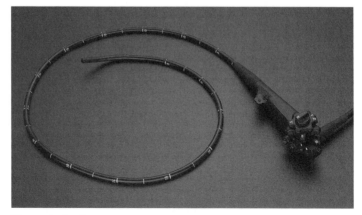

Figure 3 A colonoscope.

width of a finger) with a light and a camera mounted on the end of the tube that is inserted through the mouth or, in the case of a colonoscope, the rectum. The physician can take a biopsy by using a set of forceps passed through a thin channel in the endoscope. The forceps remove a tiny piece of tissue that is then sent to a lab for examination under a microscope by a **pathologist**. This type of biopsy is routine and painless.

Potential complications of endoscopic procedures include perforation of the bowel and bleeding. These risks are very small, and the complications are correctable. Although these procedures can be anxiety provoking, many are routine and are performed by most **gastroenterologists** on a daily basis.

Following are descriptions of the individual endoscopic procedures:

- **Upper endoscopy**

  The endoscope is passed through the mouth into the esophagus, stomach, and duodenum. This is an excellent test to help detect inflammation and strictures in the upper gastrointestinal (GI) tract and allows for a biopsy to be taken.

- **Colonoscopy**

  The colonoscope is passed through the rectum into the colon and, sometimes, into the ileum. This is an excellent test to detect inflammation and strictures in the rectum, colon, and ileum and allows for a biopsy to be taken.

- **Sigmoidoscopy**

  This procedure is performed with or without sedation; this is a "short" version of the colonoscopy and is used to examine the rectum and the first third (left side) of the colon.

Pathologist

A physician trained in the evaluation of organs, tissues, and cells, usually under a microscope; assists in determining and characterizing the presence of disease.

Gastroenterologist

A physician who specializes in diseases of the gastrointestinal tract, liver, and pancreas.

- **Proctoscopy**

  This procedure is performed without sedation, usu-ally on a special tilt table that positions the patient with his or her head down and buttocks up. In this procedure, a rigid, straight, lighted tube is used to examine the rectum. Although this procedure has mostly been replaced by flexible sigmoidoscopy, it is still an excellent test to examine the rectum.

- **Anoscopy**

  This procedure is performed without sedation, usu-ally on a special tilt table that positions the patient with his or her head down and buttocks up. In this procedure, a rigid, short, straight, lighted tube is used to examine the anal canal. This is an excellent test to examine for an anal fissure or hemorrhoids.

- **Enteroscopy**

  This procedure is performed while the patient is under sedation. A small, thin, long, flexible, lighted tube with a camera on the end, the enteroscope, is passed through the mouth into the esophagus, stomach, duodenum, and jejunum. This is an excel-lent test to detect inflammation and strictures in the upper GI tract and upper small intestine. The type of endoscope used for an enteroscopy is called an enteroscope and is longer than a traditional endoscope; thus, it can look deeper into the small intestine.

- **Capsule endoscopy**

  This procedure is performed without sedation. The patient swallows a large pill containing a camera and wears a sensor device on the abdomen. The capsule passes naturally through the small intestine while transmitting video images to the sensor, which stores data that can be downloaded to a computer for your gastroenterologist to review. Because the capsule can travel where traditional endoscopes just can't reach, this test is mostly used in evaluating patients with chronic gastrointestinal bleeding of obscure origin. While capsule endoscopy can also be used to evaluate Crohn's disease of the small bowel, other simpler tests are usually adequate and often more accurate in diagnosing and assessing the extent and severity of the disease. In addition, the capsule, which is very large, can easily become lodged in an intestinal stricture and cause an obstruction that would require an operation to remove it.

- **ERCP**

  This endoscopic procedure is performed under sedation and is used to examine the bile duct and pancreatic duct. This procedure is performed for a variety of reasons, including detecting and removing stones in the bile duct, to detect tumors involving the bile duct and pancreatic duct, and to diagnose primary sclerosing cholangitis. ERCP (endoscopic retrograde cholangiopancreatography) can also be used to dilate and place stents across strictures in the bile duct and pancreatic duct.

Histology

- **Biopsy**

  Usually performed during an endoscopy. A small piece of mucosa (the inside lining of the intestine) is removed and examined under a microscope. This is an outstanding test to characterize types of inflammation and detect dysplasia and cancer.

Laboratory Testing

Through the use of blood tests, your gastroenterologist can determine whether you are anemic, malnourished, vitamin deficient, have electrolyte imbalances, or have other abnormalities that could contribute to your symptoms. Some evidence indicates that testing positive for antineutrophil cytoplasmic antibody (ANCA) suggests that a patient has ulcerative colitis. This laboratory test is not routine and is not usually necessary to establish a diagnosis of ulcerative colitis.

Stool Testing

Stool tests are performed to rule out an infection as the cause for intestinal symptoms. Even individuals with long-standing IBD may need occasional stool testing because an infection can arise and its symptoms can mimic those of IBD. Stool testing can also be helpful in determining causes of malabsorption.

Lactose intolerance

The inability to absorb dairy products caused by a deficiency of the lactase enzyme; a type of malabsorption disorder.

Breath Testing

Breath testing can be performed to look for **lactose intolerance** and **bacterial overgrowth** as possible causes for your symptoms.

Bacterial overgrowth

A condition in which an overgrowth of normal intestinal flora occurs; usually seen in the setting of an intestinal stricture.

15. Is ulcerative colitis ever confused with other disorders?

Because the symptoms of ulcerative colitis are often non-specific and can occur in many different diseases, they are frequently confused with other gastrointestinal disorders. For example, diarrhea, which is one of the most common symptoms of ulcerative colitis, can occur in many other intestinal disorders—infectious **gastroenteritis**, such as traveler's diarrhea or giardiasis; dietary causes, such as lactose intolerance or drinking too much coffee or tea;

Gastroenteritis

An intestinal illness characterized by abdominal cramps and diarrhea; usually caused by an infection.

celiac sprue, a malabsorption disorder; an overactive thyroid; and laxative abuse. Chronic or recurrent abdominal pain may also be caused by a myriad of dysfunctions, such as gallbladder disease, **pancreatitis**, or a stomach ulcer. Rectal bleeding can occur with hemorrhoids, an anal fissure, and colon cancer. Weight loss may occur as a result of many of the conditions listed here and may also be seen with other diseases, including pancreatic cancer, **anorexia**, and **bulimia**. Last, individuals with IBS often have a combination of diarrhea and abdominal pain.

Because the symptoms of ulcerative colitis are nonspecific, a gastroenterologist may perform various radiologic and endoscopic tests to help make the correct diagnosis. However, sometimes even the tests do not give clear-cut answers. For example, infectious gastroenteritis may look almost identical to ulcerative colitis because colonic ulcers can occur in both disorders. Since many other diseases may mimic ulcerative colitis, gastroenterologists often order several tests to help establish a firm diagnosis.

16. Is it possible to be diagnosed with both ulcerative colitis and Crohn's disease?

No. Even though ulcerative colitis and Crohn's disease are two distinct diseases, one person cannot simultaneously have both diseases. A patient with Crohn's disease can have inflammation of the colon, which may be deemed "Crohn's colitis." This is not the same as ulcerative colitis. Healthcare providers often use the term "colitis" simply to refer to inflammation of the colon. which can occur in Crohn's disease, ulcerative colitis, or other forms of colitis.

DIAGNOSIS

Celiac sprue

A malabsorption disorder characterized by intolerance to gluten, which is a protein found in wheat, barley, rye, and sometimes nuts.

Pancreatitis

Inflammation of the pancreas; most often caused by gallstones, alcohol use, or as a drug side effect.

Anorexia

An eating disorder in which someone does not want to eat and has an unrealistic fear of gaining weight.

Bulimia

An eating disorder in which someone induces vomiting after eating, sometimes after eating large amounts of food, which is termed binging and purging.

Crohn's disease affects approximately 700,000 Americans. Unlike ulcerative colitis, which affects the colon, Crohn's disease can affect the entire gastrointestinal tract. Crohn's disease is limited to the small intestine in 33% of patients and the colon in 20% of patients. Both the large and small intestines are affected in the majority of patients with Crohn's disease. Inflammation in Crohn's disease can be patchy with areas of normal tissue surrounded by areas of inflammation (skip areas). There are also features found on colonoscopy and biopsy that can help your gastroenterologist distinguish ulcerative colitis from Crohn's disease. While ulcerative colitis involves the rectum, the rectum is affected in only 10 to 20% of individuals with Crohn's disease. X-rays of the abdomen can also help your gastroenterologist distinguish ulcerative colitis from Crohn's disease. Be assured that your gastroenterologist will work with you to provide a diagnosis, but you will not have both ulcerative colitis and Crohn's disease.

17. Can I ever be cured of ulcerative colitis, or will I have it for my entire life?

Remission

The state of having no active disease. It can refer to clinical remission, meaning no symptoms are present; endoscopic remission, meaning no disease is detected endoscopically; or histologic remission, meaning no active inflammation is detected on biopsy.

Unfortunately, ulcerative colitis is a disease from which you can never be completely cured. Fortunately, however, both improved diagnostic capabilities and advances in treatment enable the vast majority of individuals with ulcerative colitis to be treated successfully. Patients can enjoy long periods of **remission** in which they are symptom free. From time to time, you may meet someone who states that he or she once had ulcerative colitis but is now "cured" and has been free of symptoms and off medication for years—such patients are few and far between.

Ulcerative colitis is a chronic disease and individuals with it should expect to remain on some form of long-term therapy to maintain control of their symptoms.

18. How serious is ulcerative colitis?

Ulcerative colitis is a chronic disease and patients who have been diagnosed with ulcerative colitis take their treatment very seriously. While a small percentage of patients with a certain type of ulcerative colitis are at increased risk for developing other diseases, such as colorectal cancer, the vast majority of patients with ulcerative colitis are able to enjoy long and rewarding lives filled with work, family, friends, and leisure, no different from anyone else. Much like someone who has learned to live with the aches and pains of **arthritis**, individuals with ulcerative colitis are able to enjoy life by learning how to work around the limitations of their disease.

Arthritis

Inflammation of the joints; individuals with arthritis often have pain, redness, tenderness, and swelling in the affected joints.

PART THREE

Complications

What are some of the intestinal complications
of ulcerative colitis?

What is a stricture?

I have really bad hemorrhoids and something my
doctor calls a skin tag. Are these common in
someone with ulcerative colitis?

More . . .

19. What are some of the intestinal complications of ulcerative colitis?

Hemorrhage is abnormally heavy bleeding. Rectal bleeding is one of the cardinal symptoms of ulcerative colitis. Red blood coating or blood mixed with stool, bloody diarrhea, or passing red blood with clots is commonly found and indicates that your ulcerative colitis is active. As one would expect, rectal bleeding often leads to a great deal of worry and concern. Those with rectal bleeding sometimes wonder, "Am I going to bleed to death?" Fortunately, like a drop of red dye in a glass of water, passing blood per rectum usually looks much worse than it actually is. Most patients with ulcerative colitis who have rectal bleeding have only mild anemia. More severe anemia can be seen in chronic ulcerative colitis that has not been adequately treated and in individuals with severe **hemorrhagic colitis** that requires them to be hospitalized. Symptoms of more significant bleeding that can result in severe anemia include lightheadedness, dizziness, and fatigue. Anemia can be confirmed with a blood test to check the hemoglobin or hematocrit level, which is part of a complete blood count (CBC).

For individuals with more severe iron deficiency anemia, iron supplementation is often added. Unfortunately, iron pills can also cause gastrointestinal side effects, such as nausea, constipation, and black-colored stools. If you cannot tolerate iron pills, you can get iron intravenously (by an IV) instead. Patients who are hospitalized with severe hemorrhagic colitis and profound anemia usually require blood transfusions along with aggressive medical therapy. Massive hemorrhage occurs with severe flares of ulcerative colitis in less than 1% of patients, and treatment for the disease usually stops the bleeding. Urgent **colectomy** may be needed if the medical therapy is unsuccessful.

Toxic megacolon is one of the most serious but fortunately rare complications of ulcerative colitis.

Patients with toxic megacolon have severe abdominal pain and tenderness, abdominal distention, fever, rapid heart rate, low blood pressure, and an elevated white blood cell count. Abdominal X-rays show the colon to be markedly distended.

Toxic megacolon is potentially life-threatening and needs to be treated aggressively to prevent even more ominous complications—**sepsis**, colonic perforation with **peritonitis**, and/or shock. Patients are usually administered IV corticosteroids, IV fluids to correct electrolyte abnormalities, and nasogastric suction to remove gas from the bowel. Antibiotics are also administered to prevent sepsis.

Perforation is another serious, but rare complication. Similar to toxic megacolon, it presents with the abrupt onset of abdominal pain, tenderness and distention, fever, chills, nausea, vomiting, and an elevated white blood cell count, although, at times, the classical physical findings of perforation may be absent because of the masking effect of corticosteroids. But, most patients will still show signs of a marked deterioration in their overall clinical condition. Abdominal X-rays show that air has escaped from the bowel through the perforation and has entered into the abdominal cavity.

Colectomy
Surgical removal of the colon.

Toxic megacolon
Acute distention of the colon that usually occurs in the setting of severe colitis.

Sepsis
Severe infection that spreads through the bloodstream.

Peritonitis
Inflammation or infection of the peritoneum; this is a common complication of a perforation.

COMPLICATIONS

Patients presenting with a perforated bowel almost always undergo emergency surgery to identify the site of perforation, close the hole, or resect (i.e., remove) the diseased segment of bowel.

20. What is a stricture?

Stricture

A narrowed area of intestine usually caused by scar tissue.

An intestinal **stricture**, or narrowing, is a partial blockage of the bowel that occurs in approximately 5% of patients with ulcerative colitis. A stricture can develop from active intestinal inflammation, leftover scarring from prior inflammation, or a combination of the two. Colonic strictures are always a concern because they could also be a sign of underlying malignancy. Colonic strictures can be seen with a colonoscopy or barium enema (an X-ray with barium injected into the rectum).

21. I have really bad hemorrhoids and something my doctor calls a skin tag. Are these common in someone with ulcerative colitis?

Anus

The outside opening of the rectum.

Hemorrhoids are clumps of engorged veins in the anal canal, much like varicose veins on the legs. Hemorrhoids may be seen in individuals with either chronic diarrhea or constipation. They are believed to be formed from high pressure in the lower rectum and **anus** that develops when a person with diarrhea or constipation bears down to have a bowel movement. Also, hemorrhoids are frequently seen in women after pregnancy as a result of their bearing down to deliver. Because patients with ulcerative colitis have diarrhea, hemorrhoids may occur. During a bowel movement, the feces can scrape the hemorrhoid, causing the hemorrhoid to bleed. When blood clots within the hemorrhoids, the hemorrhoids are said to be thrombosed, which can be a very painful condition. The best therapy is to treat the underlying diarrhea or constipation. Topical therapy with steroid and anesthetic creams is often helpful as well.

Skin tags are single or multiple tags of excess anal or perianal tissue. They can develop after a **thrombosed hemorrhoid**, after anal operations, or they can form for no particular reason. As with hemorrhoids, treatment is aimed at improving the underlying bowel disorder. Local therapy with creams and ointments may also be used.

Skin tag

A piece of excess anal or perianal tissue that hangs off the anus.

Thrombosed hemorrhoid

When blood clots within a hemorrhoid, the hemorrhoid is said to be thrombosed; this can cause rectal pain.

COMPLICATIONS

31

PART FOUR

Surgery

What is the role of surgery in ulcerative colitis?

What types of operations are performed
in ulcerative colitis?

How often does ulcerative colitis
recur after surgery?

More . . .

22. What is the role of surgery in ulcerative colitis?

Although ulcerative colitis usually can be treated successfully with medical therapy, approximately one-quarter to one-third of individuals require surgery. When a person's ulcerative colitis is no longer responsive to medical therapy, the decision to perform surgery should be made jointly by you, your gastroenterologist, and your surgeon. To achieve the best outcome, all three parties should be in agreement. Often, you may want surgery because you are frustrated by your illness and feel that you won't get better. However, your physicians may encourage you to be patient, knowing from experience and extensive training that the medicine might need more time to work fully.

When a complication occurs, your doctor will determine if surgery is needed. If a bowel perforation, bowel obstruction, toxic megacolon, or uncontrollable bleeding develops, surgery may be indicated. In some situations, nonoperative therapy may be attempted, but the threshold to operate is lower and the decision is usually made quickly. Surgery for ulcerative colitis is considered curative because once the colon has been removed, the colitis does not recur.

The decision to operate is based on the individual's quality of life and not on rigid criteria. For some individuals, 8 to 10 loose bowel movements per day are severely restricting—they become housebound, cannot work, travel, go out with friends, or care for their children. For others, the same frequency of bowel movements is more inconvenient than disabling, and they are able to go about their daily activities with little or no restriction.

The type of medication the patient is taking is another factor in the decision whether to operate, because of intolerable side effects the patient may be experiencing. In addition, some patients with ulcerative colitis choose to have surgery simply to avoid having to take immune-modulating drugs. Still others prefer to exhaust all available medical options and consider surgery only as a last resort.

In patients with severe ulcerative colitis flares, toxic megacolon occurrence is approximately 5% and massive hemorrhage occurrence is about 1%. Perforation occurs in about 1% of ulcerative colitis patients without toxic megacolon. Strictures complicate ulcerative colitis in approximately 5% of patients and bowel obstruction is rarely seen. The incidence of colon cancer in ulcerative colitis varies depending on the duration and extent of the disease. It is estimated to occur in approximately 7–10% of ulcerative colitis patients after 20 years of having the disease.

23. What types of operations are performed in ulcerative colitis?

Surgery for ulcerative colitis involves removal of the entire rectum and colon, which is called a **proctocolectomy**. One question patients frequently ask is why the entire rectum and colon need to be removed rather than having a more limited resection performed of only the diseased segment as is done in Crohn's disease. A proctocolectomy is performed for two main reasons. Since the rectum is involved in ulcerative colitis, the rectum almost always needs to be removed along with the portion of inflamed colon. Then, the healthy

Proctocolectomy

Surgical removal of the rectum and colon.

35

colon must connect directly to the anus, a procedure known as a colo-anal anastomosis. This procedure is technically difficult and leads to a very poor functional outcome. Second, in ulcerative colitis after limited colonic resection, there is a very high recurrence rate, which almost always leads to removal of the remainder of the colon anyway.

Total proctocolectomy with ileostomy is one type of proctocolectomy operation performed for ulcerative colitis. It is curative, and patients can lead a long, happy, and healthy life. Unfortunately, some patients psychologically cannot accept the idea of living with an ileostomy. For this reason, whenever possible patients faced with the need for this surgery should be offered the opportunity to meet with other individuals living with an ileostomy. It is vital that patients be given the needed support from their family, physicians, stomal therapist, and support groups to help cope with this change. In the end, while prior to surgery patients often may have felt trapped by their disease, after surgery most patients feel liberated because they are finally able to work, play, travel, spend time with their family, and lead a productive life.

As an alternative to having a permanent ileostomy, patients may be given the option of having a **restorative proctocolectomy** (see **Figure 4**) in which an internal pouch, or reservoir, is created from the small bowel and is attached to the anus (remember, the small bowel and anus are healthy and are not involved in ulcerative colitis). Also known as an **ileal pouch anal anastomosis**, or **J-pouch** (because it is shaped like the letter J), this operation enables the individual to have bowel movements through the anus. This operation is usually performed in two stages. In the

Restorative proctocolectomy

Another name for an ileal pouch anal anastomosis.

Ileal pouch anal anastomosis

An operation performed mostly for ulcerative colitis in which part of the ileum is used to construct an internal pouch that is connected to the anus.

J-pouch

The same as an ileal pouch anal anastomosis; the J-pouch is named as such because the pouch is constructed in the shape of the letter J.

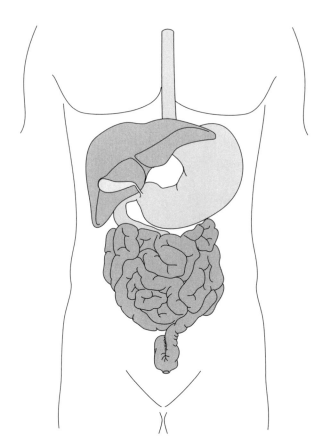

Figure 4 Ileal pouch-anal anastomosis. This is also called a "restorative" proctocolectomy.

first stage, the colon and rectum are removed down to the anus. The ileum is then used to construct a pouch that is connected to the anus. A temporary ileostomy is created to allow the ileal pouch anal anastomosis to heal. Six to eight weeks later, the patient is brought back for the second stage of the operation when the temporary ileostomy is taken down and intestinal continuity is restored. Severely ill and malnourished patients undergo the operation in three stages: stage 1—removal of the colon with formation of an ileostomy; stage 2—**proctectomy**, removal of the rectum, creation of an ileal pouch, and anastomosis of the pouch to the anus; and

Proctectomy

Surgical removal of the rectum. Individuals with Crohn's colitis or ulcerative colitis sometimes need to have a proctectomy.

stage 3—taking down of the ileostomy. Some surgeons perform the operation in only one stage, but without a temporary ileostomy to divert the fecal stream away from the ileal pouch anal anastomosis, patients run a greater risk of breakdown of the anastomosis and subsequent pelvic sepsis. If pelvic sepsis (an infection) occurs, the ileal pouch more than likely will not function optimally; eventually the pouch will need to be removed and the patient would then need a permanent ileostomy.

After surgery, patients have on average six to eight bowel movements per day of either a loose or putty-like consistency. It is common for patients to have to move their bowels one to two times each night, and some individuals have nocturnal seepage and have to wear a pad. To slow down the frequency of bowel movements and prevent dehydration, many individuals chronically take antidiarrheal medications and drink electrolyte-based fluids.

How do you decide which operation to have? This should be a joint decision among you, your gastroenterologist, and the surgeon. At times, technical factors make an ileal pouch anal anastomosis unlikely to be successful, in which case a total proctocolectomy with ileostomy would be the operation of choice. In the end, however, it often comes down to a trade-off between living with the inconveniences of an ileostomy versus the inconveniences of an ileal pouch.

24. How often does ulcerative colitis recur after surgery?

Surgery for ulcerative colitis is considered curative because once the colon and rectum have been removed, the colitis does not recur.

25. What is pouchitis, and how is it treated?

Pouchitis is inflammation of the mucosa, or inside lining, of the ileal pouch and is the most common complication after pouch surgery. Eventually occurring in up to half of all patients with a pouch, pouchitis can be mild with just an increase in frequency of bowel movements, or as severe as a full-blown flare of ulcerative colitis with watery diarrhea, **urgency**, rectal bleeding, abdominal cramps, fever, **malaise**, and **arthralgias** (joint pains). Other **extraintestinal manifestations** may be seen as well.

Urgency

The feeling that you have to move your bowels or urinate right away.

Malaise

General feeling of discomfort, illness, or lack of well-being.

Arthralgias

Joint soreness and stiffness.

Extraintestinal manifestations

Signs of Crohn's disease or ulcerative colitis that are found outside of the gastrointestinal tract.

Patients who develop these symptoms should undergo an endoscopic examination of the pouch to confirm the diagnosis. Pouchitis appears as inflamed mucosa similar to that seen in ulcerative colitis. A biopsy may also be obtained during the endoscopic examination to help further characterize the inflammation. If the pouch appears normal on endoscopic examination, the physician should look for other potential causes for the patient's symptoms. Because an intestinal infection can mimic pouchitis, stool studies should always be obtained. Crohn's disease involving the small bowel above the pouch, IBS, celiac disease, and dietary indiscretion are just some of the other possibilities.

SURGERY

The cause of pouchitis is unknown, just as the cause of ulcerative colitis is unknown. Some believe that pouchitis is from an overgrowth of bacteria in the pouch, which may be why pouchitis often improves with antibiotics. Others feel that pouchitis represents a form of IBD of the pouch. Interestingly, pouchitis is seen only after pouch surgery for IBD. It does not develop in patients who have had an ileal pouch anal anastomosis for **familial polyposis**, which is a disorder in which hundreds of precancerous polyps form in the colon, necessitating **prophylactic colectomy** to prevent colon cancer from developing.

How is pouchitis treated? Antibiotics are the most common treatment. Most patients respond after 1 or 2 weeks of therapy, although individuals with chronic or recurrent pouchitis may require long-term antibiotic therapy. In addition to antibiotics, drugs used to treat ulcerative colitis have also been used to treat pouchitis with varying degrees of success.

Not infrequently, some patients have the symptoms of pouchitis, but yet have a relatively normal-appearing pouch on endoscopy. In these cases, the patients may be experiencing spasm of the pouch, much in the way that someone with IBS experiences abdominal discomfort and diarrhea. For this reason, drugs used to treat IBS are often helpful in this setting.

Dietary indiscretion is another potential cause of pouchitis symptoms that occur with a normal-appearing pouch. Individuals with an ileal pouch have to be careful not to eat or drink substances that are known to cause diarrhea, such as caffeinated coffee and tea and too much fresh fruit and raw vegetables. In some

Familial polypsis

An inherited, pre-malignant condition in which the colon is lined with hundreds of polyps.

Prophylactic colectomy

Removal of the colon to prevent colon cancer from developing; performed in the case of familial polypsis.

individuals, it is simply the quantity of fluid intake that is the culprit. The main function of the colon is fluid and electrolyte absorption. Individuals with an ileal pouch no longer have a colon and, therefore, have less capacity to absorb fluid.

26. What are some of the other complications found after ileal pouch surgery?

Although many of the complications seen after ileal pouch surgery are those commonly found after any abdominal or pelvic operation, some are unique to the ileal pouch.

Bowel obstruction can occur after any abdominal operation as a result of the formation of adhesions, which are fibrotic bands of scar tissue that may develop within the abdominal cavity. A loop of intestine can twist around the fibrotic bands, leading to an obstruction. Unique to ileal pouch surgery, a bowel obstruction can also occur as a result of a kinking of the loop of ileum leading into the pouch itself. Whereas a bowel obstruction from adhesions usually resolves with nonoperative management, this unique type of obstruction often requires a surgical correction.

A stricture at the anastomosis between the ileal pouch and anus can also develop. Although a stricture may form at any anastomosis, they seem to occur more frequently at the pouch-anal anastomosis. A gastroenterologist can easily treat this by dilating the stricture by using either a finger or an endoscopic balloon.

An abscess or fistula can be seen following pouch surgery, as well. This can be a result of infection from an **anastomotic leak**. An anastomotic leak is when the anastomosis breaks down, usually because of an infection, which leads to intestinal bacteria leaking out, causing an even worse infection.

Female fertility has been reported to be slightly reduced after ileal pouch surgery. Male impotence and retrograde ejaculation has also been reported in approximately 2% of men after they have had ileal pouch surgery.

Finally, fecal incontinence has been reported to occur in up to half of all patients after ileal pouch surgery. Often, this can be treated with antidiarrheal drugs and bulking agents.

Anastomotic leak

Breakdown of the anastomosis, usually caused by an infection, in which intestinal bacteria leak out and cause an even worse infection.

PART FIVE

Diet and Nutrition

I find that if I watch what I eat and eliminate certain foods, I feel better. Does that mean that ulcerative colitis is caused by something in the diet and can be cured by eating the right types of food?

Is ulcerative colitis caused by a food allergy?

How does having ulcerative colitis affect my nutrition?

More . . .

27. I find that if I watch what I eat and eliminate certain foods, I feel better. Does that mean that ulcerative colitis is caused by something in the diet and can be cured by eating the right types of food?

The cause of ulcerative colitis is not known, but research has yet to prove that it is caused by something in the diet. This is not to say that diet does not play a role in this disease—it does. What you eat always has an impact on how you feel. Limiting your diet to foods that do not cause intestinal upset would make anyone feel better. This type of dietary modification is helpful for any type of intestinal problem, not just for ulcerative colitis. What is clear is that in ulcerative colitis, modifying your diet does not have an effect on the actual underlying inflammation. If you are temporarily unable to eat certain foods while in a flare or recovering from a flare, this is simply a status check that the body is not ready yet.

Though foods can't treat a flare-up of ulcerative colitis, choosing the right foods can help you deal better with the symptoms of this disease, like abdominal pain, bloating, and diarrhea. For example, a patient with ulcerative colitis who has diarrhea should avoid sugar substitutes and caffeine-containing beverages such as coffee, tea, and soda because they are known to worsen diarrhea. Milk products can be problematic for a variety of people with ulcerative colitis. Lactose intolerance is caused by a deficiency of the **lactase** enzyme, which is found normally in the small intestine. Many patients report improvement in their symptoms simply after they stop eating at fast food restaurants. So, although ulcerative colitis is not

Lactase

The intestinal enzyme responsible for the breakdown of lactose; deficiency in this enzyme leads to lactose malabsorption.

caused by anything in the diet, paying attention to what you eat can still help you feel better.

Some people get frustrated and feel like they can't eat anything they consider "healthy." Don't despair—sometimes small changes can be very helpful. For example, if you like fresh fruits/vegetables, you might substitute apples and pears with ripe banana, applesauce, and soft melon. Many vegetables can be cooked thoroughly and pureed. Always beware of big gas producers like broccoli, cauliflower, cabbage, beans, and Brussels sprouts. Often once your ulcerative colitis is under control, you can carefully expand your diet to include some foods you used to enjoy. A nutritionist is a vital member of your medical team and can help you with food choices and menu planning. He or she can also make sure you are not restricting your diet too much and missing out on vital nutrients.

28. Is ulcerative colitis caused by a food allergy?

No. No scientific evidence links ulcerative colitis to food allergies. The vast majority of adults who believe that they have an allergy to food are actually suffering from **food intolerance**, or intolerance to the method by which the food is prepared. The difference between food allergy and food intolerance is that a **food allergy** is caused by an immune system reaction, whereas intolerance does not involve the immune system. Lactose intolerance is a common example of a food intolerance. Allergies to tree nuts, peanuts, cow's milk, eggs, soy, fish, and shellfish are the most common true food allergies. Children often outgrow allergies to cow's milk,

Food intolerance

An adverse reaction to food that does not involve the immune system.

Food allergy

An immune system response to a food that the body mistakenly believes is harmful.

eggs, and soy. Those who are allergic to tree nuts, pea-nuts, fish, and shellfish usually remain allergic for life.

What should you do if you believe you are intolerant of a certain food? The most obvious measure is to elimi-nate that food from your diet and see if you feel better. Common sense dictates that if a food doesn't agree with you, avoid it! As mentioned earlier, certain foods are best avoided during a flare of ulcerative colitis. So, although many people often wonder whether gastrointestinal dis-eases are related to true food allergies, few, if any, are.

29. How does having ulcerative colitis affect my nutrition?

Most of the food that you eat is broken down in the stomach and absorbed in the small intestine. Many dis-orders can affect the small intestine and interfere with its ability to absorb nutrients properly. When this occurs, it is called malabsorption. The nutrients that may be malabsorbed include a wide variety of food breakdown products such as carbohydrates, fats, and proteins. Other essential dietary elements can also be affected, includ-ing iron, calcium, zinc, vitamin B_{12}, folate, and the fat-soluble vitamins A, D, E, and K.

Malabsorption can cause a variety of symptoms. If severe, it can cause weight loss, fatigue, and diarrhea. The diarrhea is often described as foul smelling, with greasy stools that may float in the toilet bowl (called **steatorrhea**), become difficult to flush, and leave an "oil slick" on the surface of the water. These changes in stool are often caused by malabsorption of fat, which can be measured in the stool. Again, these types of symp-toms are often found only in the later stages of severe

Steatorrhea

The presence of excess fat in the stool.

malabsorption. Most individuals with malabsorption may have only mild symptoms or no symptoms at all. Sometimes the only sign of malabsorption is the presence of anemia or a vitamin deficiency.

Your gastroenterologist is always on the lookout for signs of malabsorption and may order blood tests routinely to ensure that you do not develop major vitamin or nutrient deficiencies. Two very important nutrients are calcium and vitamin D. Malabsorption of these nutrients, which can potentially lead to osteoporosis, can be found in individuals with ulcerative colitis who take long-term corticosteroids.

Ulcerative colitis does not affect the small intestine and, therefore, does not cause malabsorption. However, someone with ulcerative colitis can become malnourished if he or she is ill with severe colitis and as a result has not been eating enough.

What is the difference between malabsorption and malnutrition? As stated earlier, malabsorption occurs when the small intestine loses its ability to absorb the nutrients and vitamins from the food that you eat. Malnutrition is an end result of malabsorption, when your body is unable to take in enough nutrients to maintain good health. Malnutrition can also happen if you don't eat enough or eat only junk foods.

30. How do I know if I should take vitamins?

Eating a healthy diet is sound advice for anyone wanting to maintain good health. For individuals with ulcerative colitis, following this advice can, at times, prove to be challenging. Patients with ulcerative colitis often live with dietary restrictions that make it difficult to eat a well-balanced diet. Because vitamins come from the various food groups, eating a restricted diet may reduce the intake of the recommended daily allotment of vitamins. Therefore, anyone who is on a restricted diet should take a daily multivitamin to supplement what he or she may be missing.

Selective vitamin deficiencies can also occur in ulcerative colitis, although it is not very common. Vitamin B_{12} is absorbed in the ileum. Accordingly, vitamin B_{12} deficiency can be found in individuals after an ileal resection. Because the deficiency is not caused by a lack of dietary vitamin B_{12}, but rather from an inability to absorb vitamin B_{12}, oral supplementation with vitamin B_{12} tablets is not effective. In this setting, vitamin B_{12} must be given through a different route—as a monthly injection or a weekly application of nasal gel. Folic acid deficiency can occur in patients taking some medications that interfere with the normal absorption of folic acid; those patients should be on a daily folic acid supplement.

Iron deficiency is commonly found in ulcerative colitis. Usually resulting from intestinal blood loss caused by an active flare of the disease, it can also be the result of reduced dietary intake. In addition to treating the active ulcerative colitis, patients are often given an oral iron supplement. Patients who are unable to tolerate oral iron, which may cause gastrointestinal side effects, can be given intravenous iron instead. Magnesium deficiency as a result of intestinal losses can be seen in patients with chronic diarrhea and can be supplemented with magnesium oxide. Trace element deficiency is rare and is found in individuals who are on home parenteral nutrition.

A common question is whether you should take any particular brand of vitamins given that many vitamins are marketed specifically for patients with ulcerative colitis or IBS and are purported to be better than typical over-the-counter vitamins. The answer is no. The vitamins you can get in any drug store are usually equal to any of the more expensive vitamins that are marketed to specific patients. You need not spend more money on brand names when the generic vitamins are equally as good.

31. I'm chronically underweight. What can I do to gain weight?

Because of dietary restrictions, patients with ulcerative colitis often find it difficult to maintain their ideal body weight. Whereas the majority of Americans are overweight and are constantly dieting, not infrequently, individuals with ulcerative colitis find themselves on the lower end of the scale trying to climb back up. There is no trick to gaining weight—simply consume more calories. However, when you have ulcerative colitis, this is easier said than done. First, if you are underweight, you should take a daily multivitamin and be checked to see if you have any particular vitamin deficiencies that need to be corrected. Next, rather than trying to gorge yourself at breakfast, lunch, and dinner, which can leave you feeling overfilled, uncomfortable, and possibly with worsening symptoms, you should instead try eating small but frequent meals. The meals should consist of nutritional and high-caloric foods. Desserts and snacks in-between meals are encouraged. Although you should never force yourself to eat, you should also not deny yourself food whenever you are hungry. Last, if this is not enough to allow you to gain the desired amount of weight, nutritional supplements are often helpful.

Many of these supplements do not contain lactose and are appropriate for those who may be lactose intolerant.

In addition to adding calories, moderate exercise with light weightlifting can also assist you in gaining weight. However, strenuous aerobic exercise can lead to further weight loss, so avoid this.

32. What foods should I eat or avoid if I have chronic diarrhea?

Diarrhea is an increase in stool volume or the frequency of bowel movements with excessive water content, occurring more than three times a day. Chronic diarrhea, defined as ongoing for more than three weeks, may be a sign of a serious problem. In addition to change in stool volume or frequency, patients with diarrhea may experience abdominal pain and bleeding with bowel movements.

Diarrhea is one of the most frustrating and embarrassing symptoms of ulcerative colitis. Treating the underlying disease is critical in managing chronic diarrhea; changes to your diet can also be helpful. Certain dietary substances are known to cause diarrhea. For instance, avoid eating foods with high fat content (such as foods that are greasy, fried, or very creamy). The fat in these foods works to speed up the contractions in your intestine that move digested food along. Caffeine, coffee, and tea also act as stimulants that can "rev up" the bowel and result in diarrhea. Fresh fruits and uncooked vegetables, high-fiber foods such as fiber-rich breads and cereals, and, at times, dairy products may also exacerbate diarrhea. Ice-cold liquids, even water, can cause cramps and diarrhea as well. In fact, too much of any type of liquid can lead to excess bowel movements. Glucose and electrolyte-based drinks, especially when diluted with water, are usually easier to absorb. Foods that may help solidify bowel movements include bananas, white bread, white rice, and cheese (if you're not lactose intolerant). See **Table 4** for a guide to which foods to eat and which foods to avoid.

Whether or not to add a fiber supplement for diarrhea can be confusing. As a general rule, high fiber of any kind is not a good idea during a flare. However, those patients who may have undergone surgery for ulcerative colitis and now have a pouch can benefit from fiber supplements that can help to thicken up the stool, reduce diarrhea, and help with leakage/incontinence. Your gastroenterologist and nutritionist can help you decide whether you might benefit from a fiber supplement.

Table 4 Foods to Include or Avoid with Chronic Diarrhea

Foods to Avoid	Foods to Include
High fat content (greasy, fried, creamy foods)	Bananas
Dairy products	White bread, white rice
Caffeine	Cheese
High-fiber foods	Boiled potatoes
Fresh fruit	Crackers, toast
Uncooked vegetables	Cooked carrots

33. Is there a specific diet that I should follow if I have ulcerative colitis?

Nutrition is an important part of everyday life. Good nutrition not only helps your body function at its best, but also promotes a strong immune system and a positive sense of well-being. This becomes more true for patients with ulcerative colitis. Naturally, everyone should strive to eat a healthy, balanced diet, especially those who have ulcerative colitis. There is no specific diet you should follow unless certain foods have made your symptoms worse.

Specific carbohydrate diet

A grain-free, lactose-free, sucrose-free diet that purportedly is beneficial in Crohn's disease and ulcerative colitis; a paucity of scientific evidence supports this claim.

The **specific carbohydrate diet** has been proposed by some as a good diet for patients with ulcerative colitis. The specific carbohydrate diet is a grain-free, lactose-free, sucrose-free diet intended for patients with ulcerative colitis and has also been suggested for patients with IBS, celiac disease, and diverticulitis. The theory behind this diet is that carbohydrates (sugars) in a normal diet act as fuel for the overgrowth of bacteria and yeast in the small intestine. This overgrowth can cause an imbalance that damages the lining of the small intestine and impairs its ability to digest and absorb all nutrients, including carbohydrates. The excess of unabsorbed carbohydrates further fuels the cycle of overgrowth and imbalance. Promoters of this diet also believe that harmful toxins are produced by the excess bacteria and yeast inhabiting the small intestine.

By consuming only certain types of carbohydrates, people using this diet hope to eliminate bacterial and yeast overgrowth. Following are certain food guidelines for the specific carbohydrate diet.

Foods to avoid:
- Canned vegetables
- Canned fruits, unless they are packed in their own juices
- All grains, including flour, corn, oats, rye, rice, spelt, and soy
- Potatoes, yams, parsnips, chickpeas, bean sprouts, soybeans, mung beans, fava beans, and seaweed
- Processed meats, breaded or canned fish, processed cheeses, soft cheeses (ricotta, mozzarella), smoked or canned meat
- Milk or dried milk solids
- Buttermilk or acidophilus milk, commercially prepared yogurt and sour cream, soy milk, instant tea or coffee, coffee substitutes, and beer
- Cornstarch, arrowroot or other starches, chocolate or carob, bouillon cubes or instant soup bases, all products made with refined sugar, agar-agar, carrageenan or pectin, ketchup, ice cream, molasses, corn or maple syrup, flours made from legumes, baking powder, medication containing sugar, and all seeds

Foods to eat:
- Fresh and frozen vegetables and legumes (raw or cooked)
- Fresh, raw, or dried fruits
- Fresh or frozen meats, poultry, fish, and eggs
- Most nuts, including all-natural peanut butter
- Natural cheeses, homemade yogurt, and dry curd cottage cheese

Although this diet may seem like a simple, natural way to "treat" an intestinal disorder, it has yet to be proved scientifically to help people with ulcerative colitis. Although the "Foods to eat" list provides a healthy alternative to many items on the "Foods to avoid" list, several comments need to be made about the diet as a whole. First and foremost, special diets should never be used as treatments for ulcerative colitis and should never replace medications that have been proven to provide benefit. Although healthy diet choices should be a part of everyone's lifestyle, eliminating too many foods from a diet can be cumbersome. Patients who may also be lactose intolerant should avoid milk products. Certainly, fresh foods are a healthier alternative to canned or processed foods. However, during an ulcerative colitis flare, too many fresh fruits and vegetables can create a big fiber load for the small intestine and colon. While the specific carbohydrate diet is a reasonable nutrition plan with some modification, you should tell your gastroenterologist or nutritionist about this and any other special diets you may be considering. The bottom line is to beware of special diets that make big promises.

34. Do all patients with ulcerative colitis have lactose intolerance?

Lactose intolerance is a very common problem for many people. It is caused by a deficiency of the lactase enzyme, which is found normally in the small intestine. Lactose is a major ingredient in dairy products such as milk, ice cream, yogurt, and cheese. There are also many less obvious sources of lactose. Did you know lactose can even be found in certain pills and deli meats? However, some nutritional supplements, even though they may look like a milkshake, do not contain lactose.

Symptoms of lactose intolerance include diarrhea, bloating, **flatulence**, and abdominal cramps after ingesting a lactose-containing product. Often, the higher fat content of milk products like ice cream can also contribute to these symptoms. The only treatments are lactose avoidance, taking supplemental lactase enzymes before eating or drinking a dairy product, or using products like milk/soy milk and ice cream that are specially made lactose-free. Remember that if you are lactose intolerant, you'll need to find other ways to supplement your calcium and vitamin D intake because you will no longer be getting them from your diet.

Because the lactase enzyme is found in the small intestine, even healthy patients who get a "stomach bug" or viral gastroenteritis can have problems digesting lactose products for a little while until the lining of the bowels can heal. It is reasonable to eliminate dairy from your diet for a week or two after a diarrheal illness until the level of lactase enzyme can return to normal.

There are two ways to diagnose lactose intolerance. The most common way is to avoid dairy for 1 week and see if the cramps and diarrhea go away. Then drink a glass of milk and see if they recur. If you still are not sure whether you are lactose intolerant, your doctor can order a **lactose breath test** as a more objective measurement. Sugars (such as lactose) not absorbed properly in the small intestine make their way to the colon where they are metabolized by bacteria. These bacteria give off hydrogen, which quickly crosses the lining of the colon into the bloodstream and can be measured in the breath.

The day before the lactose breath test, you are instructed to avoid high-fiber foods that can cause an unusually high baseline level of hydrogen in the initial breath

Flatulence

Excessive gas in the digestive tract.

DIET AND NUTRITION

Lactose breath test

A test used to diagnose intolerance to lactose.

samples. Brushing your teeth also helps to decrease excess bacteria in your mouth that can also cause abnormally high baseline hydrogen readings. At the start of the test, you blow into the machine and the hydrogen level is measured. Then, you are instructed to drink a solution that has a high amount of lactose. Subsequent breath measurements for hydrogen are taken at 15- to 30-minute intervals over a 2-hour period. The total rise in hydrogen from the baseline measurement is then calculated. If this rise is greater than 20 parts per minute (ppm), lactose intolerance may be present. Certain situations such as recent antibiotic use, gastroenteritis, or small bowel bacterial overgrowth can cause the results to be inaccurate.

PART SIX

Related Conditions

Can ulcerative colitis affect parts of my body other than just my bowels?

How can ulcerative colitis affect my skin?

I often get little sores in my mouth, especially when my ulcerative colitis is active. Are these related, and what can I do about them?

More . . .

35. Can ulcerative colitis affect parts of my body other than just my bowels?

Ulcerative colitis can affect many different parts of your body (see **Table 5**). These are referred to as extraintestinal manifestations because these effects are found outside of the gastrointestinal tract. Extraintestinal manifestations are also called **systemic** symptoms because they reflect a process involving the body as a whole (a system), as opposed to local symptoms, which occur just in the intestinal tract. Systemic symptoms include fatigue, weight loss, anemia, and sometimes low-grade fevers. Extraintestinal manifestations can also be more localized to a specific organ. Organs that can be affected include the skin, eyes, joints, bones, kidneys, urinary tract, reproductive system, **gallbladder**, liver, and circulatory system. Although this list is quite long, extraintestinal manifestations do not occur in every patient. Approximately 25% of individuals with ulcerative colitis may develop one or more of the extraintestinal manifestations. Joint symptoms, such as arthritis, are the most common and are often seen together with skin and eye symptoms.

Systemic

A process that involves the whole body, as opposed to a localized process; for example, fatigue is a systemic symptom, whereas lower back pain is a local symptom.

Gallbladder

A small sac, adjacent to the liver, where bile is stored.

Table 5 Extraintestinal Manifestations of Ulcerative Colitis

Common	Uncommon
Anemia	Blood clots
Joint pains	Nerve damage
Skin rashes	Primary sclerosing cholangitis (liver disorder)
Mouth ulcers	
Gallstones	Lung disease
Kidney stones	Pancreatitis (inflammation of the pancreas)
Eye problems	
Growth retardation in children	Pericarditis (inflammation around the heart)

We do not yet know what causes extraintestinal manifestations to develop, just as we do not know the cause of ulcerative colitis. The leading theory is that because this disease is believed to be a result of a defect in the immune system, this same defect could potentially lead to inflammation in other areas of the body in addition to the gastrointestinal tract. Why certain people develop extraintestinal manifestations and others do not is still unknown.

The presence of extraintestinal manifestations often provides additional clues as to the level of activity of the underlying ulcerative colitis. This is because, in many cases, extraintestinal manifestations often reflect ongoing intestinal inflammation that may not be apparent to either you or your gastroenterologist. In fact, some individuals use their extraintestinal manifestations as a signal as to when they are about to have a flare.

In general, effective treatment of the underlying disease usually leads to resolution of the extraintestinal symptoms. Some of the extraintestinal manifestations, however, run a course independent from the underlying ulcerative colitis and do not improve along with improvements in the intestinal symptoms. It is also important to remember that systemic symptoms are sometimes a result of a drug-induced side effect and not from an extraintestinal manifestation.

Now you know why your gastroenterologist asks a long list of questions concerning many aspects of your overall health and does not focus just on your bowels at each visit. Ulcerative colitis involves not just the gastrointestinal tract, but can affect many different areas of the body as well. Indeed, at times the extraintestinal manifestations can be severe enough to overshadow a person's underlying intestinal symptoms. It is for this reason that you should inform your healthcare provider when you are having new symptoms, even if they seem unrelated to your bowel disease.

36. How can ulcerative colitis affect my skin?

The two most common types of skin rashes seen in individuals with ulcerative colitis are **erythema nodosum** and **pyoderma gangrenosum**. Both rashes are very distinctive. Erythema nodosum appears as a painful, tender, reddish-purplish bump that occurs mostly on the shins; it can be found over the rest of the legs and arms as well. Erythema nodosum is a sign that your ulcerative colitis is active.

Unlike erythema nodosum, pyoderma gangrenosum can appear at any time and is not related to the activity of the underlying intestinal inflammation. Pyoderma gangrenosum is found most commonly on the legs and adjacent to an ileostomy or colostomy, although it can appear anywhere on your body. It starts as a red, inflamed area of skin usually smaller than the size of a dime. This inflamed area soon forms a punched-out, sharply demarcated ulcer with a raised reddish-purplish border. Pyoderma gangrenosum exhibits what is called the **pathergy phenomenon**. This is an unusual dermatologic condition in which a skin ulcer can get bigger and deeper as a result of even minor trauma, such as abrasive cleaning or pulling off a sticky dressing. For this reason, you should never attempt surgery on pyoderma gangrenosum. Because of the pathergy phenomenon, it can get large enough so that it takes months to heal. Pyoderma gangrenosum is not a common rash and,

Erythema nodosum

Skin condition characterized by tender reddish-purple nodules that can occur on the shins, legs, and arms in patients with IBD; can also be associated with other diseases.

Pyoderma gangrenosum

A skin ulcer that can occur in patients with IBD anywhere on the skin, but most commonly is found on the extremities and immediately adjacent to a stoma.

Pathergy phenomenon

An unusual dermatologic condition that occurs in pyoderma gangrenosum, in which even minor trauma can cause a skin ulcer to become bigger.

therefore, can be difficult to diagnose by the untrained eye. Any individual with ulcerative colitis who develops an ulcer on the skin should be considered to have pyoderma gangrenosum until it is proved otherwise.

Several treatments are available for pyoderma gangrenosum. First and foremost, the ulcer should be bandaged with a nonstick dressing so as to avoid trauma when you change the dressing. First-line therapy usually consists of topical therapy with a corticosteroid ointment and cromolyn sodium. Topical cyclosporine has also shown good results. Corticosteroids can also be injected directly into the ulcer, but this approach is limited to use only on small ulcers and is not used as often as topical therapy. If topical therapy and/or corticosteroid injection is not successful, systemic therapy with oral or IV corticosteroids and various immune-modulating drugs has been found to be beneficial. In addition, even though pyoderma gangrenosum may occur in an individual whose ulcerative colitis is in remission, it can also appear in someone with an active flare. In such a case, the active inflammation should be treated aggressively.

37. I often get little sores in my mouth, especially when my ulcerative colitis is active. Are these related, and what can I do about them?

Sometimes patients with ulcerative colitis can develop small, painful sores in the mouth called **aphthous ulcers**. They can be very bothersome and appear much like canker sores. Infrequently, much larger ulcers can develop. Topical oral anesthetics can be helpful to numb the pain. A topical corticosteroid is often mixed in with

Aphthous ulcers

Small ulcers that can occur in Crohn's disease or ulcerative colitis.

the anesthetic. Usually the oral ulcers occur when the intestinal inflammation has become more active. Mouth sores can also develop as a side effect of some of the medications used to treat ulcerative colitis. Antibiotics, for example, can cause **thrush**, which is an oral fungal infection. Also, the immune-modulating drugs can leave your body susceptible to viral infections such as the herpes simplex virus (HSV) or cytomegalovirus (CMV), both of which can cause sores on the lips and inside the mouth.

Thrush

Oral (mouth and throat) fungal infection; appears as a whitish plaque on the tongue and on the inside lining of the mouth.

38. My joints are often stiff and sore. Is this related to my ulcerative colitis?

Individuals with ulcerative colitis often complain of having sore and stiff joints. The medical term for soreness and stiffness in the joints is arthralgia. Arthritis is when the joints are actually inflamed—painful, red, swollen, and warm. These joint symptoms can be divided into two categories: those that affect the central or spinal joints (back, pelvis, hips), and those that affect the peripheral joints (shoulders, elbows, wrists, fingers, knees, ankles, toes).

Peripheral arthralgias may be seen in up to 20% of individuals with ulcerative colitis. These patients often experience painful, stiff joints throughout their body. A single joint or several joints can be affected at the same time, or the pain can migrate from one joint to another. Sometimes a true arthritis can be seen with a red, hot, and swollen joint. Arthritis associated with ulcerative colitis is different from both **osteoarthritis** (so-called wear-and-tear arthritis) and rheumatoid arthritis. The type of arthritis associated with ulcerative colitis is a nondestructive form of arthritis, meaning that it does

Osteoarthritis

Arthritis caused by natural wear and tear on the joints; commonly occurs in older individuals, but can also be found in younger athletes as a result of years of trauma.

not permanently damage the joints. This is different from osteoarthritis and rheumatoid arthritis that do lead to joint destruction.

For this reason, it is important for your healthcare provider to investigate any new joint symptoms you have because they may be caused by a variety of illnesses. If a single joint is red, hot, or swollen, it could mean the joint is infected. **Gout** is another condition that can cause pain in a single joint, often the big toe. In gout, uric acid crystals form and become concentrated in the joint fluid, causing inflammation and pain. Your healthcare provider may want to remove a sample of fluid from the joint with a small needle to send for laboratory analysis and examination under a microscope to rule out these other causes of joint pain.

Peripheral arthralgias associated with ulcerative colitis usually mirror the activity of the underlying bowel disease. In other words, the joint pains often develop as a result of an active flare, sometimes just before a flare is about to happen.

Central (spinal) arthralgias occur in approximately 5% of people with ulcerative colitis. The joints that are most affected include those of the lower spine and pelvis, specifically the sacroiliac joints within the pelvis. Patients may develop pain or stiffness in the lower back that is worse in the morning upon waking and improves with activity throughout the day. Unlike peripheral arthralgias, arthritis affecting the central joints can lead to permanent damage, when joints fuse together in the vertebral column, as well as in the sacroiliac region. Central arthritis is also different from peripheral arthralgias in that it is not necessarily associated with the level of bowel activity. In fact, central arthritis can show up

RELATED CONDITIONS

Gout
Type of arthritis characterized by uric acid crystal deposition in the joints; often presents as a red, swollen, painful big toe.

years before bowel symptoms occur. Treatment is targeted toward helping control the arthritis symptoms. Range of motion exercises, physical therapy, and moist heat applied to the back can be helpful.

39. Is it true that ulcerative colitis can also affect my eyes?

Eye disorders associated with ulcerative colitis are among the most serious of the extraintestinal manifestations. Left untreated, they can result in permanent damage, including scarring and blindness. It is for this reason that you and your healthcare provider should be quick to consult an ophthalmologist for prompt diagnosis and treatment of any eye symptoms (as discussed here). The ophthalmologist will use a slit lamp test (a microscopic view of the inside structures of the eye) to detect different abnormalities. Sometimes corticosteroid eye drops are used as well. Regardless, any new eye symptoms must be evaluated promptly because delay in treatment can cause lasting damage to the eyes.

Episcleritis

Inflammation of the white of the eye.

Iritis

Inflammation of the iris, which is the colored part of the eye.

Uveitis

Inflammation of the uvea, which is the central portion of the eye.

The three most common eye disorders associated with ulcerative colitis are **episcleritis**, **iritis**, and **uveitis**. These names correspond to different structures in the eye that have become inflamed. Episcleritis refers to inflammation of the white of the eye; iritis refers to inflammation of the colored part of the eye; and uveitis refers to inflammation of the central portion of the eye. Often, the tiny blood vessels of the eye become inflamed, causing them to dilate or expand, which is what causes the eye to become red. Other symptoms include pain, sensitivity to light, and blurred vision. These ocular disorders often occur along with arthritis and erythema nodosum. Usually the problem will affect only one eye at a time. You should contact your gastroenterologist immediately to be evaluated. Often the ophthalmologist will prescribe steroid drops to alleviate the inflammation and prevent any damage to the eye.

Other problems that affect the eyes, such as cataracts and **glaucoma**, can be side effects of the long-term use of corticosteroids. Needing reading glasses as you get older, on the other hand, has nothing to do with ulcerative colitis—it's simply part of the natural aging process.

Glaucoma

Increased pressure within the eye.

40. How does ulcerative colitis cause you to become anemic?

Anemia is a condition that occurs when the body is depleted of red blood cells. The two main causes of anemia are loss of blood and decreased production of red blood cells. Blood loss is most commonly caused by gastrointestinal bleeding. Other potential sources of blood loss include a bleeding ulcer or bleeding from **diverticulosis**. A variety of illnesses can cause anemia from decreased production of red blood cells, including iron and vitamin deficiencies, lead poisoning, bone marrow problems, chronic kidney failure, and certain blood disorders such as **sickle cell anemia** and **thalassemia**. Some medications may also cause anemia. Caveat: Anyone over the age of 50 who develops new-onset iron deficiency anemia should be checked thoroughly for an underlying gastrointestinal cancer such as colon cancer as a possible cause.

Diverticulosis

A condition that develops when pouches (diverticula) form in the wall of the colon.

Sickle cell anemia

An inherited blood disorder that can cause anemia.

Thalassemia

An inherited blood disorder that can cause anemia.

Symptoms of chronic anemia include tiredness, pale skin, shortness of breath on exertion, and decreased exercise capacity. This happens because red blood cells deliver oxygen to the various tissues and organs of the body. As the number of red blood cells decreases in anemia, the body does not get enough oxygen to work at full capacity. If you have underlying heart disease, chest pain and shortness of breath can be important signals that your heart is under excessive stress and that the anemia needs to be corrected immediately with a blood transfusion. Severe anemia can lead to a rapid pulse, decrease in blood pressure, and episodes of passing out. When this occurs, an immediate blood transfusion is usually needed. However, the majority of patients with ulcerative colitis who have chronic anemia do not need blood transfusions, but usually get better with folate, B_{12}, or iron supplementation. Bleeding from ulcerative colitis does not usually cause significant anemia and is rarely severe enough to require a blood transfusion.

PART SEVEN

Other Questions and Concerns

Is it safe to have a baby if I have ulcerative colitis?

Can ulcerative colitis affect fertility in men?

Can I take ulcerative colitis medications
while I am breastfeeding?

More . . .

41. Is it safe to have a baby if I have ulcerative colitis?

This disease most commonly affects young men and women during their childbearing years, so naturally many individuals with ulcerative colitis are concerned about whether they can safely have children. Pregnancy itself does not appear to pose any increased risk to women who have ulcerative colitis as compared to those who do not. However, studies have shown that women who have active, poorly controlled ulcerative colitis during pregnancy are more at risk for miscarriage, premature delivery, and stillbirth. For women whose disease is in remission, there is still a small risk for premature delivery and low birth weight. That being said, women with ulcerative colitis in remission generally have normal pregnancies and deliver healthy babies. It is important to note, however, that even for the average healthy woman without ulcerative colitis, there is still a 2–3% chance of having a complication during pregnancy. In other words, there is still some degree of risk inherent in any pregnancy.

42. Can ulcerative colitis affect fertility in men?

The inflammation from ulcerative colitis generally does not cause fertility problems in men. However, it is possible that one of the drugs commonly used to treat ulcerative colitis can cause a reversible decrease in sperm count, reduced sperm motility, and abnormal sperm shape. If you are taking any medication for ulcerative colitis, check with your healthcare provider about its effect on fertility. It is likely that another effective medication can be substituted. Men who have had pelvic surgery may have a low risk of infertility and choose to bank their sperm beforehand.

43. Can I take ulcerative colitis medications while I am breastfeeding?

Many of the medications listed as safe during pregnancy are also considered safe for use during breastfeeding. There are some medications that are not recommended for breastfeeding mothers—ask your healthcare provider which ones these are. This can be a very emotional issue for some women and should be discussed at length either prior to or early on in the pregnancy. It is important to remember that if you have a flare, you may become too ill to breastfeed. So, although you may prefer to breastfeed and should be allowed to if you can, bottle-feeding may be the safest option if the alternative is an ulcerative colitis flare in a new mother.

44. If I have ulcerative colitis, what is the chance that my children will have it?

Some studies suggest if either parent has IBD, the chance their child will have IBD is approximately 2-9%. One study reported that if both parents have IBD, the chance their child will have IBD is 33%. In general, the risk is higher with Crohn's disease than with ulcerative colitis. So while there is a risk, just because you have ulcerative colitis doesn't automatically mean that your kids will have it, too.

Several genes have been identified as being associated with ulcerative colitis. One is called the NOD2/CARD 15 gene, which has more than 60 variations. It is important to remember, though, that although these genes are involved in ulcerative colitis, they are only part of the story. The NOD2/CARD 15 gene is believed to play the role of a permissive gene, meaning that the gene cannot cause the disease by itself, but can help facilitate the expression of ulcerative colitis. In other words, even if you carry one of these genes, you will not automatically develop ulcerative colitis. Rather, ulcerative colitis may be caused by a combination of genetic influences and an environmental trigger, such as a bacterium.

45. Does stress affect ulcerative colitis?

Based on scientific evidence, the following statements can be made:

1. Emotional stress alone cannot cause a person to develop ulcerative colitis.
2. Emotional stress alone cannot induce a flare of ulcerative colitis.
3. There is a no higher incidence of major psychiatric illness in patients with ulcerative colitis than the general population.

That being said, many people with ulcerative colitis still believe that major life stressors coincide with a flare. Certainly, stress can make it harder to deal with ulcerative colitis when it is flaring. Additionally, a patient with ulcerative colitis, or any chronic illness, who also suffer from depression, have a more difficult clinical course than a patient who is chronically ill without depression. In addition, some of the corticosteroids that are used to treat ulcerative colitis may cause severe mood swings, irritability/anger, tremulousness, insomnia, and depression.

Individuals under stress with or without a history of ulcerative colitis commonly suffer gastrointestinal symptoms such as cramps, bloating, constipation, and/or diarrhea. This is similar to getting a headache due to stress. If these symptoms occur frequently and in certain patterns, they are likely due to IBS. The body often senses and reacts to changes in environment long before our conscious mind registers them. Unfortunately, those with ulcerative colitis often have IBS, too. IBS symptoms, such as the ones mentioned here, can often occur despite the fact that the ulcerative colitis is in remission. Additional strategies can be used to help with IBS symptoms.

PART EIGHT

Communicating With Your Gastroenterologist

What should I discuss with my gastroenterologist?

How often should I see my gastroenterologist?

What should I do about new problems and questions?

More . . .

46. What should I discuss with my gastroenterologist?

Open, honest communication is the key to a true partnership with your gastroenterologist. In fact, research has shown that successful communication between a patient and a clinician can lead to better patient outcomes (e.g., better emotional health, better symptom resolution, and better functional and physical status). For your gastroenterologist to provide the best possible care for you, he or she needs to know more than the facts of your illness. In order to decide what treatment is best for you, he or she may look at your particular case, you personally, your general philosophy about your health, and your ability to cope with illness.

Should I keep a daily journal?

Keeping a daily journal is a good idea, as it allows you to track your symptoms and provides you and your gastroenterologist with information about the course of your disease. If you are taking medication, a daily journal may show whether or not the medication has taken effect. People with ulcerative colitis are encouraged to track the number and quality of daily bowel movements (bloody, firm, etc.), weight loss, severity of gastrointestinal inflammation/cramping, diet, nausea/vomiting, and level of stress. While neither stress nor diet can cause ulcerative colitis, or even cause a flare, both diet and stress can exacerbate symptoms that are already present.

5-ASAs

Aminosalicylates are medications used to treat the inflammation associated with IBD; they come in oral and topical forms.

Biologic agents

A group of therapeutic medications that include monoclonal antibodies.

What types of medications are used to treat ulcerative colitis?

Several types of medications are used to treat patients with ulcerative colitis. The major types include the **aminosalicylates (5-ASA) drugs**, immune-modulating drugs, corticosteroids, antibiotics, and **biologic agents**.

Aminosalicylates

The 5-ASA (aminosalicylates) drugs are usually taken orally and act to reduce inflammation, but they do not affect the immune system. In addition to oral preparations, other 5-ASA treatments include **retention enemas** and **suppositories**.

Corticosteroids

Corticosteroids are potent anti-inflammatory drugs and are used in oral, rectal, and intravenous (IV) forms. Corticosteroids reduce the inflammation associated with ulcerative colitis. Although very effective for short-term use, corticosteroids have limited effectiveness for long-term use and are associated with a number of side effects and complications.

Immune-modulating drugs

Immune-modulating drugs (also known as **immunomodulators**) are used in patients who do not respond to anti-inflammatory medications, such as aminosalicylates. These types of drugs work by modulating/suppressing the body's immune system to prevent the inflammation associated with ulcerative colitis. By suppressing the immune system, one of the potential complications of immune-modulating drugs is an increase in the risk of infections. Patients on immunomodulators need regular monitoring of their blood to look for decreased red and white blood cells, as well as elevation in the liver function tests (which are possible side effects of the medications). Individuals on these types of medications should also contact their healthcare providers at the first signs of an infection.

Biologic agents

Biologic agents are used in patients who do not respond well to other drugs. They block a specific protein in the

Retention enema

A process of instilling liquid (usually oil-based) into the rectum, where it is retained for several hours, to soften stool.

Suppository

A small plug of medicine, often cylindrical, that is inserted into the vagina or anus, and is designed to melt at body temperature.

Immuno-modulators

A class of drugs that modulates or suppresses the immune system.

body, called tumor necrosis factor-alpha (TNF-alpha) which plays a role in the immune-mediated inflammation associated with ulcerative colitis. Because these drugs suppress the body's immune system, they also reduce the body's ability to fight infections. TB and other types of serious infections have been associated with biologic agents, as well as, some cancers. Patients are screened and monitored for tuberculosis, other serious infections, and the development of cancer. Patients should talk to their doctor about the risks and benefits of these types of medicines.

Antibiotics

Antibiotics are also used to treat infections that may develop in patients with ulcerative colitis.

Pain relief

Acetaminophen is the preferred pain medication for use in patients with ulcerative colitis. You should not use narcotic medications chronically, given the potential for addiction. Patients with chronic pain unrelated to active colitis might benefit from a referral to a comprehensive pain center.

Will I need surgery?

Whether or not you can continue to treat your ulcerative colitis with medical therapy alone is a decision that should be made jointly by you, your gastroenterologist, and your surgeon. There are several factors to consider and to achieve the best outcome, all three parties should be in agreement. Make sure you understand the reasons why your gastroenterologist is or is not recommending surgery for your ulcerative colitis. Ask questions in order to better understand the recommendation.

Should I get a second opinion?

Most patients with ulcerative colitis have a mild form of the disease that can easily be managed by a gastroenterologist; however, some individuals have a more aggressive form of the disease. In particular, patients with extensive colitis and ongoing symptoms, despite the use of steroids or immunomodulators, are at increased risk for complications and might benefit from a second opinion.

Keep in mind that your gastroenterologist wants you to get better and wants you to take an active role in your ongoing care. Don't be embarrassed to ask for a second opinion about treatment options, prognosis, or any aspect of your healthcare plan—it does not mean you don't trust your gastroenterologist, it just means you want to learn more about your disease. You may be surprised to find that some insurance companies recommend or encourage patients to get second opinions. Some people choose to consult with a second gastroenterologist when:

- They are considering surgery
- Their clinician prescribes a new medication
- They are not seeing an improvement in symptoms despite repeated visits to their gastroenterologist
- They want to learn more about alternative treatments

There are multiple places to look when you are researching gastroenterologists' credentials to find one to consult for a second opinion. Hospital Web sites list faculty members and their credentials, health insurance companies have lists of resources in your community, and even your gastroenterologist can suggest other clinicians for you to see. Another resource is the Crohn's and Colitis Foundation of America (CCFA), which provides a list of gastroenterologists with expertise in treating ulcerative colitis.

Ask your clinician to send your medical records to the gastroenterologist that will be providing a second opinion. If you will be bringing the records with you, it will be helpful to have notes from office visits, results from colonoscopies, and pathology reports. Also, for reference, plan to bring along original biopsy slides, X-rays, CT scans, and MRI scans. Ask the gastroenterologist prior to your appointment, as they may be able to provide you with a list of items they would like you to bring.

47. How often should I see my gastroenterologist?

You and your gastroenterologist will work to develop your treatment plan, which will include how often to schedule appointments. Certainly contact his or her office if new problems arise, or keep a list of questions and concerns to bring to the next visit.

48. What should I do about new problems and questions?

Try to limit new problems and questions to the most important ones. Written descriptions and your own opinion of the diagnosis will suggest other questions by the clinician. Write down the name or diagnosis of the problem.

It may also improve your understanding if you ask to have everything explained in lay (nonmedical) terms. Be certain you fully understand your diagnosis. Ask your gastroenterologist's office if they have printed information on the new subject to give you and ask what the procedure is to get results of testing and consultations. For example, there may be a special telephone number to call to get results.

49. Will I be given a treatment plan?

You and your gastroenterologist should create a treatment plan together. After you and your provider have developed the treatment plan, follow it closely. And be honest—do not say you will follow the treatment plan if you will not (e.g., avoiding caffeine). Furthermore, be sure the treatment plan takes into account your lifestyle, religious, and cultural preferences. Make sure you know which follow-up steps to take, when to call and why, and with whom you should speak (e.g., provider, receptionist, nurse). If you notice problems or side effects, notify your gastroenterologist immediately. If you wish to change methods of treatment, then express this to your gastroenterologist. You need to be a partner in developing the treatment plan.

50. Where can I find a support network?

There are many resources available for people diagnosed with ulcerative colitis. A list of useful organizations and their contact information is show in **Table 6**. The Crohn's and Colitis Foundation of America (CCFA) has an information resource center that provides accurate and current disease-related information. There are local CCFA chapters throughout the country that run educational programs as well as support groups. You can find a support group near you by searching the CCFA Web site or calling their toll-free number. There are also a few online support groups available. The Web sites *www.dailystrength.org* and *www.supportgroups.com* both have dedicated ulcerative colitis online support groups.

Table 6 Resources on Ulcerative Colitis

Name of Organization	Web site	Phone Number
American College of Gastroenterology	http://www.acg.gi.org	301-263-9000
American Gastroenterological Association	http://www.gastro.org	301-654-2055
Crohn's and Colitis Foundation of America	http://www.ccfa.org	800-932-2423
The Foundation for Clinical Research in IBD	http://www.MyIBD.org	
HealthCentral	http://www.healthcentral.com/ibd/	703-302-1040
International Ulcerative Colitis Group	http://www.ihaveuc.com	
IBD Support Foundation	http://www.IBDSF.com	310-552-2033
National Digestive Diseases Information Clearinghouse	http://digestive.niddk.nih.gov	800-891-5389
Ulcerative Colitis Resources	http://www.livingwithuc.com	
United Ostomy Association of America	http://www.ostomy.org	800-826-0826

#

5-ASAs: Aminosalicylates are medications used to treat the inflammation associated with IBD; they come in oral and topical forms.

A

Abscess: A walled-off collection of pus; in Crohn's disease, an abscess is most commonly found around the anus or rectum, but can occur anywhere in the body.

Anastomotic leak: Breakdown of the anastomosis, usually caused by an infection, in which intestinal bacteria leak out and cause an even worse infection.

Anorexia: An eating disorder in which someone does not want to eat and has an unrealistic fear of gaining weight.

Anus: The outside opening of the rectum.

Aphthous ulcers: Small ulcers that can occur in Crohn's disease or ulcerative colitis.

Arthralgias: Joint soreness and stiffness.

Arthritis: Inflammation of the joints; individuals with arthritis often have pain, redness, tenderness, and swelling in the affected joints.

B

Bacterial overgrowth: A condition in which an overgrowth of normal intestinal flora occurs; usually seen in the setting of an intestinal stricture.

Bile duct: A channel through which bile flows from the liver to the intestines.

Biologic agents: A group of therapeutic medications that include monoclonal antibodies.

Biopsy: Usually performed during an endoscopy, a small piece of mucosa (inside lining of the intestine) is removed and examined under a microscope; an excellent test to characterize types of inflammation and detect dysplasia and cancer.

Bulimia: An eating disorder in which someone induces vomiting after eating, sometimes after eating large amounts of food, which is termed binging and purging.

C

Celiac sprue: A malabsorption disorder characterized by intolerance to gluten, which is a protein found in wheat, barley, rye, and sometimes nuts.

Colectomy: Surgical removal of the colon.

Colonic transit time: The time it takes for stool to travel from the beginning of the colon (the cecum) to the rectum.

Colonoscopy: An endoscopic procedure in which a small, thin, flexible lighted tube with a camera on the end is passed through the rectum into the colon and, at times, into the ileum; an excellent test to detect inflammation and strictures in the rectum, colon, and ileum, and one that allows for a biopsy to be taken.

Crohn's disease: A disease characterized by inflammation of the gastrointestinal tract which can affect any area of the gastrointestinal tract.

D

Diverticulosis: A condition that develops when pouches (diverticula) form in the wall of the colon.

Duodenum: The first part of the small intestine just beyond the stomach.

Dysplastic cells: Cells that are in a state of abnormal growth or development.

E

Episcleritis: Inflammation of the white of the eye.

Erythema nodosum: Skin condition characterized by tender reddish-purple nodules that can occur on the shins, legs, and arms in patients with IBD; can also be associated with other diseases.

Extraintestinal manifestations: Signs of Crohn's disease or ulcerative colitis that are found outside of the gastrointestinal tract.

F

Familial polypsis: An inherited, premalignant condition in which the colon is lined with hundreds of polyps.

Fistula: A tunnel connecting two structures that are not normally connected; examples include a fistula between the rectum and vagina (rectovaginal fistula) or the colon and bladder (colovesicular fistula).

Flatulence: Excessive gas in the digestive tract.

Food allergy: An immune system response to a food that the body mistakenly believes is harmful.

Food intolerance: An adverse reaction to food that does not involve the immune system.

G

Gallbladder: A small sac, adjacent to the liver, where bile is stored.

Gastroenteritis: An intestinal illness characterized by abdominal cramps and diarrhea; usually caused by an infection.

Gastroenterologist: A physician who specializes in diseases of the gastrointestinal tract, liver, and pancreas.

Genetic predisposition: An inherited trait that makes one more likely to develop a disease.

Glaucoma: Increased pressure within the eye.

Gout: Type of arthritis characterized by uric acid crystal deposition in the joints; often presents as a red, swollen, painful big toe.

H

Hemorrhage: Abnormally heavy bleeding.

Hemorrhagic colitis: Colitis that has been complicated by severe bleeding.

Hemorrhoids: Engorged veins found in and around the rectum and anus. Often they bleed and can cause rectal pain. Blood can become clotted within the hemorrhoids, which is a condition called thrombosed hemorrhoids.

I

Ileal pouch anal anastomosis: An operation performed mostly for ulcerative colitis in which part of the ileum is used to construct an internal pouch that is connected to the anus.

Immune dysregulation: Failure of the body to appropriately regulate the immune system; this lack of regulation is believed to be integral to the development of Crohn's disease and ulcerative colitis.

Immune-mediated disease: A condition that results from abnormal activity of the body's immune system.

Immune system: An internal network of organs, cells, and structures that work to guard your body against foreign substances, such as infections.

Immunomodulators: A class of drugs that modulates or suppresses the immune system.

Inflammation: A process characterized by swelling, warmth, redness, and/or tenderness; can occur in any organ.

Iritis: Inflammation of the iris, which is the colored part of the eye.

J

J-pouch: The same as an ileal pouch anal anastomosis; the J-pouch is named as such because the pouch is constructed in the shape of the letter J.

L

Lactase: The intestinal enzyme responsible for the breakdown of lactose; deficiency in this enzyme leads to lactose malabsorption.

Lactose breath test: A test used to diagnose intolerance to lactose.

Lactose intolerance: The inability to absorb dairy products caused by a deficiency of the lactase enzyme; a type of malabsorption disorder.

Left-sided colitis: Ulcerative colitis that involves the left side of the colon.

M

Malaise: General feeling of discomfort, illness, or lack of well-being.

O

Osteoarthritis: Arthritis caused by natural wear and tear on the joints; commonly occurs in older individuals, but can also be found in younger athletes as a result of years of trauma.

P

Pancolitis: Extensive ulcerative colitis; ulcerative colitis that extends beyond the left colon.

Pancreatitis: Inflammation of the pancreas; most often caused by gallstones, alcohol use, or as a drug side effect.

Pathergy phenomenon: An unusual dermatologic condition that occurs in pyoderma gangrenosum, in which even minor trauma can cause a skin ulcer to become bigger.

Pathologist: A physician trained in the evaluation of organs, tissues, and cells, usually under a microscope; assists in determining and characterizing the presence of disease.

Perforation: A rupture or abnormal opening of the intestine that allows intestinal contents to escape into the abdominal cavity.

Perianal: The area adjacent to the outside of the anus; common site for abscess and fistula formation.

Peritonitis: Inflammation or infection of the peritoneum; this is a common complication of a perforation.

Prevalence: The number of people affected by a disease in a population at a specific time.

Primary sclerosing cholangitis: Inflammation and scarring of the bile ducts within the liver; can occur in ulcerative colitis and Crohn's disease.

Proctectomy: Surgical removal of the rectum. Individuals with Crohn's colitis or ulcerative colitis sometimes need to have a proctectomy.

Proctitis: Inflammation of the rectum.

Proctocolectomy: Surgical removal of the rectum and colon.

Proctosigmoiditis: Ulcerative colitis limited to the rectum and sigmoid colon, and not involving the descending colon.

Prophylactic colectomy: Removal of the colon to prevent colon cancer from developing; performed in the case of familial polypsis.

Pyoderma gangrenosum: A skin ulcer that can occur in patients with IBD anywhere on the skin, but most commonly is found on the extremities and immediately adjacent to a stoma.

R

Remission: The state of having no active disease. It can refer to clinical remission, meaning no symptoms are present; endoscopic remission, meaning no disease is detected endoscopically; or histologic remission, meaning no active inflammation is detected on biopsy.

Restorative proctocolectomy: Another name for an ileal pouch anal anastomosis.

Retention enema: A process of instilling liquid (usually oil-based) into the rectum, where it is retained for several hours, to soften stool.

S

Sedation: Also called conscious sedation, or moderate sedation; sedation is a form of moderate anesthesia in which the patient is given medication to induce a state of relaxation.

Patients under sedation are sleepy and are less likely to feel discomfort.

Sepsis: Severe infection that spreads through the bloodstream.

Sickle cell anemia: An inherited blood disorder that can cause anemia.

Sign: Objective evidence of disease; a characteristic that can be identified on physical examination or by a test.

Skin tag: A piece of excess anal or perianal tissue that hangs off the anus.

Specific carbohydrate diet: A grain-free, lactose-free, sucrose-free diet that purportedly is beneficial in Crohn's disease and ulcerative colitis; a paucity of scientific evidence supports this claim.

Steatorrhea: The presence of excess fat in the stool.

Stricture: A narrowed area of intestine usually caused by scar tissue.

Suppository: A small plug of medicine, often cylindrical, that is inserted into the vagina or anus, and is designed to melt at body temperature.

Systemic: A process that involves the whole body, as opposed to a localized process; for example, fatigue is a systemic symptom, whereas lower back pain is a local symptom.

T

Tenesmus: Intense rectal spasm, usually caused by inflammation.

Thalassemia: An inherited blood disorder that can cause anemia.

Thrombosed hemorrhoid: When blood clots within a hemorrhoid, the hemorrhoid is said to be thrombosed; this can cause rectal pain.

Thrush: Oral (mouth and throat) fungal infection; appears as a whitish plaque on the tongue and on the inside lining of the mouth.

Toxic megacolon: Acute distention of the colon that usually occurs in the setting of severe colitis.

U

Ulcerative colitis: A disease characterized by inflammation of the colon.

Upper endoscopy: A procedure in which a small, thin, flexible, lighted tube with a camera on the end is passed through the mouth into the esophagus, stomach, and duodenum; an excellent test to detect inflammation and strictures in the upper gastrointestinal tract that allows a biopsy to be taken.

Urgency: The feeling that you have to move your bowels or urinate right away.

Uveitis: Inflammation of the uvea, which is the central portion of the eye.